Women of Color

Women of Color

The Multicultural Guide to Fashion and Beauty

DARLENE MATHIS

Foreword by Carole Jackson,
Bestselling author of *Color Me Beautiful*

ONE WORLD

BALLANTINE BOOKS
NEW YORK

Copyright © 1994 by Darlene Mathis
Foreword copyright © 1994 by Carole Jackson

Library of Congress Cataloging-in-Publication Data

Mathis, Darlene
  Women of Color: The Multinational Fashion Guide/Darlene Mathis.
      p. cm.
   ISBN 0-345-38929-8
   1. Beauty, Personal
   2. Afro-American woman—Health and hygiene
   i. Title
   RA778.M377 1994
   646.7′2—dc20   94-15715
                                                        CIP

Produced by Book Builders/Judd Publishing Inc.

Art direction, jacket, and text design by Robert Hickey

Manufactured in the United States of America

First Edition: September 1994

10 9 8 7 6 5 4 3 2 1

"With that Sister Eagle unfurled her wings,
and my, she did fly."

—Rev. Nawanna Miller,
from "Sister Eagle"

Acknowledgments

I am truly blessed with friends and clients who have been both loyal and faithful to me during the years I was developing into a more positive woman of color.

I wish especially to thank my two daughters for their understanding: To Halston, who says she forgives me for not being able to take turns as a "carpool mom" or go rollerskating with her. And to Tameka, who blesses my efforts even when I'm not able to find time to take those long rides and share secrets like we used to and who says she really didn't mind my moving her from dorm to dorm during her first semester (even though she probably did). I love you both, deeply and forever.

Thanks also to Carole Jackson, my mentor, for being a true friend. We may be of different heritages but we share a commonality as mothers, sisters, and friends.

To Kathleen Hughes, my editor and agent for her patient, sincere, and undivided direction. There were times when I did not think I could put my years of experience on paper. Kathleen brought out the author in me, and I will never forget her honesty and support.

To Rue Judd, the motivator and negotiator. I will always remember our first New York trip for our BIG interview. She cheered me on and gave me the nudges I needed to make this book a reality.

To Robert Hickey, my art director, for his way of making you feel special. He has an eye and style for how a woman should look and a gift and vision for the future. As art director, his talent is evidenced throughout this book.

To my friends, Wendell Gardner, Jr., and Lyn Yager-Alexander, for being so supportive and understanding.

And to Random House/Ballantine Books, Joelle Delbourgo, and Elizabeth Zack, for believing in me and allowing me to express my talents through creating *Women of Color* for a market of forgotten women.

Special thanks also to: Barbara Diggs-Brown, Pamela Perkins Brown, Wenonah Cohen, Diana Tardd, Constance Viere de Cunba, Helen Wesserman, Donald Leege, Blenna Cunningham, Doris Lyles, Fred Rigney, and Arthur Pakolski.

Table of Contents

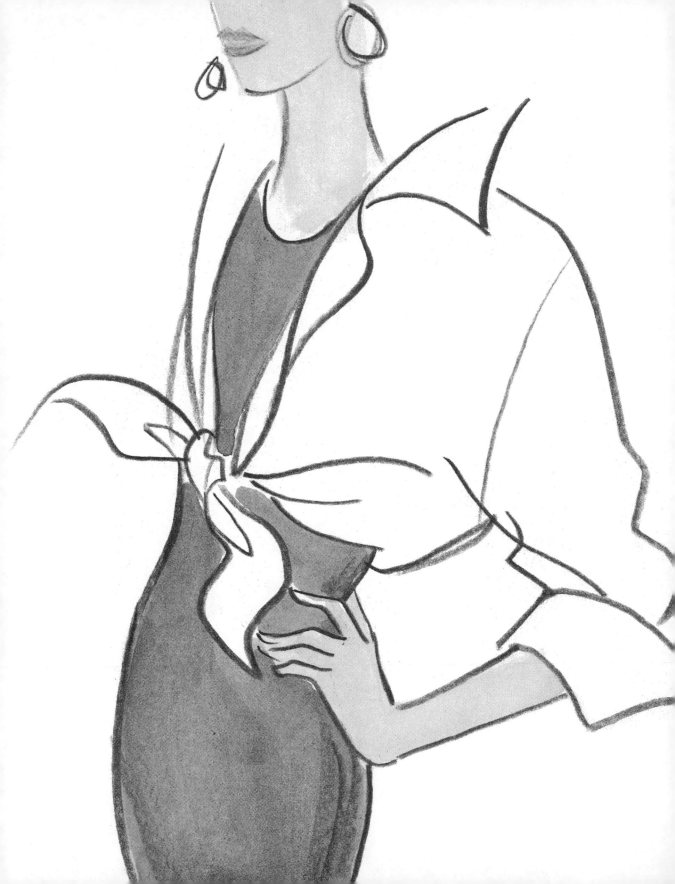

Foreword

When Darlene Mathis attended one of my early Color Me Beautiful training programs, she was determined to be the best beauty consultant in the business. Darlene already had a polished image and an extensive and impressive background in the beauty business, but she wanted to learn firsthand what the seasonal color system was about. She was skeptical. Why not just match your lipstick to your clothes, the way the cosmetics industry advises? Darlene watched and analyzed my every move. She wanted proof.

When I showed Darlene that the fuchsia outfit she was wearing would look more exciting and harmonious with silver jewelry, rather than the gold she was wearing, she gave a slight frown—but I could see the wheels turning in her mind. We draped her, and she could see how her Winter colors brought her natural beauty to life. Her eyes lit up with the glow of revelation as she began to understand how this miraculous color system works.

Since then we have become the best of friends ... and inveterate researchers over the years. Although a large percentage of her clients were African, Asian, and Hispanic Americans, and most often fell into the Winter classification, Darlene soon began to challenge the original Color Me Beautiful palettes, which were designed primarily for Caucasian skin tones. She could see that there are warm-skinned Springs and Autumns and softer cool-skinned Summers among all people. She experimented. Simultaneously, as I traveled to Japan, Europe, Bermuda, and all over the United States, I began adding, subtracting, and adjusting colors from the palettes to better suit the varieties of ethnic skin tones. Darlene and I frequently conferred and compared notes.

Darlene now presents in her book a more flexible seasonal color system that reflects the diversity of all peoples. There are women all over the world, in the United States and Canada, in Mexico and Colombia, Pakistan and Nigeria, China and Japan, Israel and Kuwait, Argentina and Zimbabwe, who are moving into new jobs and new positions of authority. They need to know how to build a wardrobe that reflects their growing authority, and they need to know how to do it on a budget. Plus, they want to look their absolute best. (Who doesn't!)

Darlene has built a significant list of clients, some in high public places, others eager to get there, others who serve quietly behind the limelight. She has helped each of them discover a world of colors that make them look and feel better and more confident than at any time in their lives. She's colored their hair, cut and designed it for them, suggested makeup, and built them a wardrobe that works. From a new place in the world, they write back to tell her their happy news. They come back for regular makeovers; they love her.

I, too, love Darlene. She is a special lady—warm, caring, loving, and so supportive. She has the gift of making others feel good about themselves. Her work is in her heart, as she truly sees the beauty God has created in every woman.

In this book, Darlene is helping a new generation of women realize their potential by recognizing their special seasonal color palette and learning to use it to build a smashing wardrobe appropriate to their aspirations. She knows they can do it, and color can pave the way—helping them to organize their wardrobe, shopping, and beauty time, and age gracefully. Darlene is the makeup and beauty expert for her time.

I salute Darlene Mathis and the world of women whose beauty has never before been so appreciated. This is your time. Use the colors of the seasons to take you wherever you want to go.

With love,

Carole Jackson

Darlene Mathis

Introduction

I was happy and quite successful managing my own hair and skin salon with a clientele of lovely women who were embarking on various careers and were aware of the importance of a positive image. But I knew I had the potential to do much more—for them and for myself. So, I decided to broaden my career and become an image consultant to offer them makeup and wardrobe advice.

I had heard a lot about color, but I didn't understand why all the fuss about colors, palettes, hues, palettes, seasons, palettes, ugh! I knew that there *must* be a reason so many people were committed to the seasonal color theory, so I took the Color Me Beautiful training.

At the risk of oversimplifying, the seasonal color theory uses nature to organize colors into four pretty palettes: cool, clear Winter; soft, cool Summer; warm, rich Autumn; and warm, bright Spring. It's not the temperature that's important, it's the undertone of our skin. Winters and Summers have cool blue and purple undertones; Springs and Autumns have golden yellow undertones. Each palette contains the colors that best suit the skin tones and hair and eye colors for that particular season. Once you know your seasonal palette, shopping, wardrobe planning, and makeup application become simpler and, frankly, a lot more fun.

Meeting Carole Jackson, the founder of Color Me Beautiful, during my training was a wonderful experience. Carole is a Winter, and she wore the vivid colors that look great on her. She was so captivating that I wanted to be as much in charge of my audience as she is and present the same authoritative image to my clients. I walked into the training instinctively knowing that I felt and looked better in whites and blacks. But I also thought I could wear gold accessories. Well, I was stripped of all the gold accessories I wore into the room that day. I was taught that I am a Winter and look better in cool colors and silver accessories. I was amazed and excited to learn all the dimensions of the seasonal color theory, and I developed a new way to wear my gold jewelry and look fantastic!

During the training, I was draped in Autumn and Winter colors. When the warm colors of Autumn were closest to my face, I looked dull, and the blemishes on my skin were more pronounced. Basically, I looked horrible. When Winter's cool colors were draped closest to my face, I looked radiant, elegant, and a lot younger. I felt as if I had had a face-lift.

I became more convinced that the seasonal color theory could work for me and *my* clients. From that moment on, I became a lifetime believer in the seasonal color theory.

I went back to my Monday Mornings beauty salon and business as usual—but with one significant change. I applied the seasonal color theory to my clients, who are all women of color. There I found, to my dismay, that some of the principles didn't quite apply to my richer-hued customers. In the original book, *Color Me Beautiful*, all Africans, Asians, and Hispanics were classified as cool Winters. I, on the other hand, was discovering a world of bright-hued women who were Springs, Autumns, and Summers.

I continued working with women of color, creating color palettes for them and encouraging them to use makeup colors I developed. As I suspected, I found women of every hue, representing all ethnic groups, who were Springs, Autumns, and Summers, as well as Winters. When I called Carole Jackson and shared my findings with her, she was intrigued by what I had discovered and encouraged me to continue my research.

For the last fifteen years, I've continued to develop my "Women of Color" theory that applies to the vast majority of the earth's population—people of color. We are a universe of colors. Women of color come in many shades and are looking for their own identity through the color theory. We all share a common bond in being women, mothers, daughters, and sisters. We are all searching for ways to look and feel good and succeed. And we are all distinctive because of our cultural backgrounds.

Unfortunately, many of us have been programmed to see blond and blue-eyed as the epitome of beauty. For years, those were the attributes of women winning the beauty pageants and endorsing the beauty products. But what about the fashion-conscious American of Asian and African heritage? What about Bermudian and Bahamian women? What about Hispanic and Native American women? What about darker hued women all over the world?

When we go into bookstores and look in the health and beauty sections, we find how-to books for blond and brunette women only. There is little or nothing for women of color. And that's why I've written this book for you.

From the beginning of my color career, I have counseled many women who have been my clients ever since. Throughout this book you'll hear their stories and others about women who represent each of the seasons and who have followed different career paths. Identify first with the woman who most closely represents your career choice. Let her story inspire you.

Let's start with Carmen. She is a nurse of Puerto Rican heritage who was color analyzed as a Winter but was not happy with her palette. Aggravated by her previous experience, she came to Monday Mornings to be redraped, saying she felt gloomy in white and she could not find a lipstick color that suited her Winter wardrobe. I asked her to relax a bit, we chatted, and I learned as much as possible about her and her lifestyle. I discovered the mistake that had been made in her original color analysis. At the time, her hair was dyed jet black, but her skin tone was very warm. She is a Spring whose wrongly colored hair had given her an artificial appearance, and almost wrecked her self-esteem.

I covered her hair with a clear plastic bag and draped her in Winter colors. Then I put a medium dark-brown wig on her and draped her in Spring colors. Technically she could wear some of Autumn's colors because of her warm skin, but because she is petite, most of the Autumn colors are a little overpowering for her. After the draping session, we tried several shades of lipstick, blushes, and shadows. This session confirmed Carmen as a Spring. She left feeling renewed and good about how she looked. I suggested she pass the Winter wardrobe she had worn to a friend and exchange the items she had not worn for new Spring ones.

I gave Carmen a small palette of the colors I developed for Spring. For comfort and security, she always takes it with her when she shops to insure she purchases *only* colors that she can wear. I received a letter from Carmen recently. She said she is very happy and continues to receive a lot of compliments. She has become more productive and motivated now that she knows she is a Spring.

Vivian, a flight attendant from Taiwan, came to my salon because she was bored with her appearance. She is a tall size twelve with long, medium-brown hair with golden highlights. She is a true Autumn, and I gave her new colors to brighten her life. We started with her makeup, adding russet red lipstick and a soft russet blush. She had been wearing orange-reds,which were great for her, but she wanted more choices. I suggested she try a greenish eye shadow and dark-brown eye pencil and mascara. After I finished her makeover, I redraped her and added some fun to her life. We added teal, peach, and red-violet to be used as accessory colors for her scarves, blouses, and sweaters. She still likes black, and we allowed her to use it in skirts, slacks, and blazers, but never next to her face. Vivian walked away feeling very confident and highly motivated by her new look.

Anita is a tall, intelligent, and charming Colombian Winter who looked washed out in the gray she insisted upon wearing because of her executive level position. She directs a division in the federal government's national mortgage agency, and she was afraid to strike out and wear color during her work day. Previously held by men only, her position requires that she be heard and respected by her male counterparts, and she mistakenly equated gray with authority.

We had a long session during which I learned a lot about her personality. A true Winter, Anita enjoyed the center stage of an executive, but she did not want to take advantage of the drama that is a natural part of her. We began by helping her understand how Winter's strong colors—red, purple, and black—can be both dramatic and understated.

I helped her find her strongest color, which is red, and she was amazed to see that a red suit, tailored just right, is perfect for the business world. In this color she has presence and captivates her listeners. Now she walks and talks with authority, and she's not afraid of fire.

Anita now says that I have a sixth sense about what a woman needs and an uncanny ability to know when she is ready for a change, before she articulates it.

When Cydney arrived for her first wardrobe enhancement session, I was immediately struck by her beauty. She is a forty-seven-year-old teacher who looks as young as some of her art students. She received a color analysis more than five years before our meeting, and she is a strong Summer African-American, with gentle brown eyes and thick brown hair that hangs midway down her back.

She wanted to add a little more sophistication to a fairly substantial and, I found, tasteful wardrobe. She wanted to look a little more "worldly" than her students, and, at the same time, retain her youthful appearance. We had such fun! First, I encouraged her to take advantage of two of her strong colors—white and rose; this was easy because, as an artist, she appreciated the color theory. We used these colors for shirts, body suits, and leggings to complement her major pieces.

Second, we varied her style a little. She is tall and thin and can wear the long lines of leggings under today's longer, maxi-jackets. We purchased a few pairs of leggings and just the right jacket in another strong Summer color—navy. She is stunning also in long sarong skirts, and we added a couple of those for variation and to be worn with oversized shirts over bodysuits.

Cydney is really happy with the work we did, and we shop for her often, adding smaller items regularly and major pieces less frequently. She says that her new, more sophisticated look sets her apart from her students, and makes her feel great! It's just the edge she needed.

Throughout these pages, you will find many stories like these. You'll find clients and models who remind you of yourself or someone you know. Share their stories. You'll be challenged and motivated by the colors, illustrations, and fashion ideas. Try them; they will keep you busy for a long while. Encourage someone else to try them. Most of all, this book is for us, women of color. Enjoy!

CHAPTER 1

For The Artist in You—Color

"Beauty is only skin deep!" Well, that's far enough for us because your skin tone is going to tell you what your seasonal color palette should be. And your skin will provide the canvas upon which you—the artist—will apply the colors of your special palette. But let's find your palette first.

We Come in All Colors

Heritage and nature have done the real work for you already. Women of color—African Americans, Arabs, Asians, Native Americans, Hispanic Americans, East Indians, and others—come in all colors of the rainbow with their hair, eye, and skin tones. Your job is to discover your natural colors and then to develop the skills of an artist to enhance that natural beauty.

But don't worry. You don't have to wield a paint brush. For you, heritage has already prepared your canvas—giving you a unique skin color among the vast array of skin tones and hair and eye colors that we women of color flash on the world. Look in the mirror. You may be blue-black with green eyes, warm coffee brown with brown eyes, peach with brown eyes, rosy with blue eyes, golden with hazel eyes, or black on black.

It's Time

It is time to take the initiative, a proactive stance. Traditionally, we women of color have felt that in order to gain social acceptance and economic success, we had to work toward a look reflecting European beauty. We tried to lighten our skin with makeup, and we colored, bleached, and straightened our hair. In the past, women who were biracial couldn't even *find* the correct cosmetics! There weren't any made for them because they were not white enough or had too much brown or yellow in their skin. What a waste! Well, by the year 2000, a majority of the world's population will be biracial, and cosmetics companies *will* be competing for their business. But for now, if we can discover our seasonal color palette, we'll find that cosmetic, clothing, hair, and accessory choices can be ours to command.

Color Will Open Your Horizons

Take a look at the palettes beginning on page 37. You'll notice that nature has provided the same colors or hues for us all, but has altered them for each season so that no season has an exclusive on a particular color. The *intensity* and *shade* of colors in each palette are what make your season unique. In other words, each seasonal palette includes variations of the same colors. In each season, you will find colors that may appear, at a glance, to look like another seasonal palette; look again. The color will be a lot stronger for Autumns, a lot brighter for Springs, a lot clearer for Winters, and a lot softer for Summers. And whatever your race, you'll find that your unique coloring can be reflected in any one of these four seasons.

Winters and Summers are those cool customers who dance in the primary color spectrum—red, blue, and yellow—but Summer needs pink or rose, light blue and yellow (softer, more muted shades of those cool tones), while Winter sparkles in true red, bright blue, and deep, clear yellow. Autumn and Spring like warm, rich secondary colors— orange, green, and purple—but Spring needs the lighter shades— shrimp, lime, and periwinkle—to bloom.

The colors in your palette will always compliment you, and you should never tire of them. There may be some colors in your palette that you don't like as much as others. Do try them some time, but start with the ones you like most, or the ones you already have a lot of in your wardrobe. Later you'll undoubtedly find that you want to experiment with all the colors in your palette. It has such a full spectrum of colors appropriate for every occasion, and every season of the year. Have fun. Color opens your horizons; *it doesn't limit them.*

You may find colors you like in another season. Don't be tempted, and don't feel cheated. The truth is there are probably colors in every season that look all right on you. But that is not the point of this book. I want you to look *sensational*. Your own personalized colors are guaranteed to do that for you. With them, you won't lose a thing.

Your palette is rich with colors that are sophisticated, others that are playful. You will find colors that are exotic and colors that are elegant. There are colors that say, "Let's get down to business," and others that say, "Let's just get down."

They are all there, and combined in the 1 + 1 Professional Wardrobe combinations outlined in Chapter 3, these colors will take you anywhere, anytime.

Don't Let It Manage You!

Wardrobe coordination becomes a lot easier when you know your season. It allows you to become a better manager of your closet and drawers. You can tie together colors that blend and contrast with those basic blacks, blues, and browns. Coordinating your wardrobe spares you the time pondering what to wear for an occasion and allows you the freedom to mix and match. It also saves you money because you won't duplicate. Have you ever wondered *why* you have so many lipstick and eye shadow colors? Well, knowing your season will give you two dominant shades of lipstick, four shades of eye shadow, and four shades of blush that go with all you wear.

Shopping Will Be Easy

Shopping is *easy* when you first discover the added advantage of having your own palette of colors. Your palette is *portable*. You can carry it with you when you shop. The right decisions will be easier when you can hold your color samples against your prospective purchase. It they don't have the same clarity or softness or richness or shine, don't buy. Accessories will suddenly become a joy and not a job to choose. They'll pull all the colors together, and become the frame for the image you'll present.

A Woman of Color Who Pulled It All Together

My client and dear African-American friend Jewel Jones of Anchorage, Alaska, is an example of someone who knows how to make the possibilities of her palette limitless. Jewel, a social worker, is an

Autumn who is full of zest. I see her twice a year at Monday Mornings for "the works"—makeup, hair, and wardrobe-building. She loves earth tones and looks fantastic in browns, oranges, and greens. She spends close to four hours in my salon. We change her hair color to an updated, fresh shade from her palette and give her a new haircut. Then I bring out new makeup colors for her to try. Finally we pick over all the exciting new earrings, scarves, sunglasses, and other accessories that can add to her existing wardrobe.

I met Jewel through a business associate who insisted that Jewel reroute her trip back to Anchorage to meet me. It has been twelve years since our first meeting. Jewel still calls when she hears of a new product line and gets my opinion before she invests in any new cosmetic color line that features colors and styles for African-American women.

She writes me after each visit to say, "Each year since we've met, I have come back to Washington at least twice a year for both business meetings and the pleasure of seeing you and the magic of the beautiful transformations you create. I'm always a new person when I leave the salon." I hope you'll feel this way after reading this book!

Let's Have Some Fun

We are now ready to select your palette, but remember: Discovering your seasonal palette does *not* mean you will be wearing colors suited only to a particular time of year. The seasonal names are designed to direct you to a particular *palette*. You become an artist; from here on, *you* will make all the decisions about what shades and intensity of colors will suit the time of the year and best express your lifestyle.

Okay, let's have some fun and create a new, beautiful woman of color: you!

Your Season...Your Palette

This is a test. Yes, but it's not difficult at all, and it's one which you'll be thrilled to pass. In fact, it is a test for which you have been preparing since birth. By the end of this chapter, you will have a palette from which you can choose the outfits, makeup, and accessories that make the statement you want to make. You are on your way to having much more fun with fashion, and if you don't think shopping is fun, you will at least be on the way to enjoying the *efficiency* of this new way of shopping.

Your color test has two phases. First, you'll identify the colors you are already wearing with success. Second, you'll analyze the coloring of your skin, hair, and eyes. When the results are in, you will know your season and have an exciting palette of colors from which to work miracles.

I suggest that you complete the test on pages 45-56, and then peruse the beautiful color section that follows this page: You'll come to love the colors that embody your season—and you!

Text continues on page 45

What is the seasonal color theory?

Get ready to find out what colors make you look and feel your very best.

The seasonal color theory uses nature to organize those colors into four pretty palettes: cool, clear Winter; soft, cool Summer; warm, bright Spring; and warm, rich Autumn. It's the undertone of your skin we are looking at here. Winters and Summers have cool blue and purple undertones, while Springs and Autumns have warm yellow and golden undertones.

Everyone has her own unique coloring, although one of the four palettes contains the colors that will most flatter your natural beauty. Look at this family of gorgeous women. Grandmother Darvine is a Winter, mother Elizabeth is an Autumn, and daughters Erica and Catherine are Summers. Each wears one of her best colors: Grandmother in royal purple, Mother in butterscotch, and Erica and Catherine in their summer navy.

Now look at the groups of colors on the next pages and discover your seasonal palette.

Which Is Your Season?

*A*rrange by color the clothes in which you receive the most compliments. Look at your clothing colors and at the groupings of colors below.

The Cool Seasons

Winter

Black

Sapphire Blue

Clear Red

Emerald Green

Deep Lemon

Summer

Charcoal Gray

Baby Blue

Rose

Apple Green

Light Lemon

*W*hich group best reflects the dominant colors in your wardrobe? Which group do you like best?

The Warm Seasons

Autumn

Dark Brown

Teal

Orange

Olive Green

Gold

Spring

Warm Beige

Turquoise

Shrimp

Lime

Bright Yellow

Jenny

Anna

Sandy

Winters

Winters have blue, pink-rose, or purple undertones that give their skin its cool drama. They range from pearly white to blue-black, but can even be olive skinned. Winters have very deep eye color — warm brown, black, or hazel (a combination of gray-brown and blue). Their hair is black to dark brown, ranging from medium brown to extremely dark, sometimes with red highlights. Winters are more likely to gray prematurely and their gray ranges from a very attractive blue-gray to pure white.

Jenny, Anna, and Sandy represent three distinct Winter women of color. **Jenny** is a Chinese-American with bone white skin, shiny blue-black hair, and arched eyebrows above her flashing onyx eyes. She looks terrific in true clear red with a silver necklace.

Anna is a blue-black African American with dark black hair and eyes. She is a woman of deep drama in brilliant emerald green and striking silver jewelry.

Sandy is a Hispanic beauty with a deep rosy beige complexion, dark brown eyes, and hair with red highlights. In her clear Carribbean blue shirt, she reflects the vividness of her heritage.

Winter women of color have the intensity of coloring — pure whites, black, deep reds, and blues — that symbolize the season of snow and roaring fires and the happy celebration of the Winter solstice.

The Winter Palette

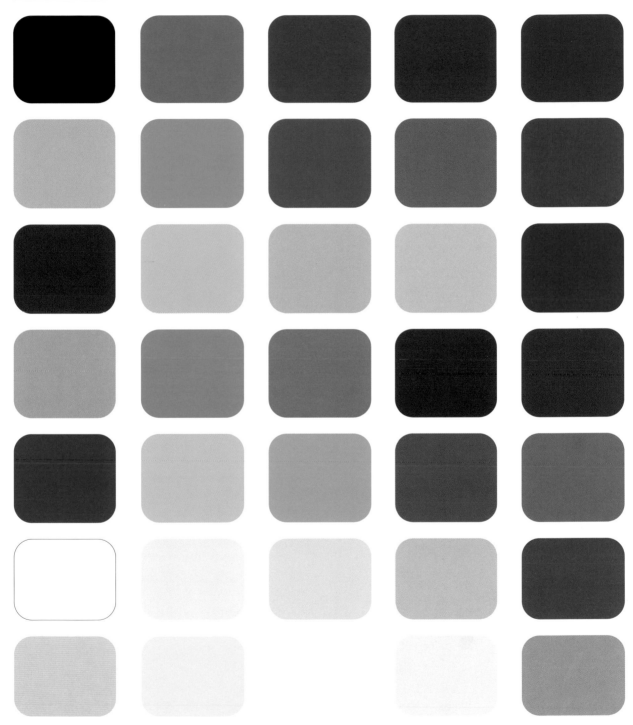

The Winter palette includes both cool neutrals and cool bright colors. Use your neutrals for business and the others for nonbusiness clothing and accessories. For more about wardrobe building with your colors see page 78.

Mita

Naomi

Altomease

Summers

Most Summer women have pinkish skin or a little pink color on their cheeks. Hispanic, Asian, and African-American Summer women have pale beige, very light to olive, skin tones — all with a calm blush of rosy-blue. Their skin is often translucent. Summer eyes are cool blue or gray blue or softest brown. A few Summers have green eyes mixed with brown. As children, Summers frequently have light brown to blonde hair. But as they mature, it darkens to light ash brown or ash blonde. Most Summer women of color become brunettes.

Mita, Altomease and Naomi are lovely examples of Summers. **Mita,** with soft brown hair and eyes, set off by a rosy complexion, is perfect in dove gray with delicate silver jewelry.

Cool olive-skinned **Naomi** with medium brown hair and eyes is enchanting in palest pink silk.

And brunette **Altomease** has a cool beige complexion with a gentle rose blush that is enhanced by her soft pink sweater.

Summer women are gentle romantics, soft as a summer breeze, calm as a beach at high noon. They are good listeners and good friends.

The Summer Palette

The Summer palette includes both cool neutrals and cool muted colors. Use your neutrals for business and the others for nonbusiness clothing and accessories. For more about wardrobe building with your colors see page 80.

Marcia

Karen

Paula

Autumns

The skin of Autumn women can be ivory or peach, golden beige or brown, and can even appear yellow. Autumns have little color in their cheeks, so blushes make them seem even more glamorous. Their hair is full of golden or auburn highlights, and is dark brown or dark blonde, copper brown, auburn, or red. Autumn's eyes are warm brown, golden brown, green, blue, or hazel. Blue-eyed Autumns usually have golden or brown flecks in the iris which makes their eyes look steel-blue from a distance.

Marcia, Paula, and Karen are Autumn women of distinct beauty. **Marcia,** with her long dark blonde hair, light golden brown skin, and hazel eyes is luxurious in red-orange.

Karen has golden brown skin, deep golden brown hair with red highlights, and golden brown eyes. Dressed in gold, with gold jewelry, she is truly a vision.

Paula is an auburn-haired, peach-skinned, hazel-eyed beauty. In olive green she is radiant, while any other season would look muddy.

A harvest moon, the bright hues of change, and a sense of abundance — all make Autumn a special season. The Autumn woman is earthy, sensuous, sophisticated, and assertive. She makes a strong impact on those around her with her vigor and energy.

The Autumn Palette

The Autumn palette includes both warm neutrals and warm muted colors. Use your neutrals for business and the others for nonbusiness clothing and accessories. For more about wardrobe building with your colors see page 82.

Tomara

Yolande

Edda

Springs

Springs' complexions are ivory, peach, golden beige, or warm brown. African-American Springs are light and golden, with clear skin. Asian Springs have very light to ivory skin. Hispanic Springs have natural warm color on their forehead and cheeks. Springs have golden blonde, medium light red, or golden to medium brown hair. Some Springs have bright, clear, natural blonde hair. Others have medium to dark brown hair with or without red highlights. Spring eyes are clear, light to amber brown, blue, or green with yellow flecks.

Tomara, Yolande, and Edda are lovely representatives of Spring's bright beauty. **Tomara's** light golden beige skin, warm brown eyes, and light reddish brown curls dance in Spring's clear yellow.

In Spring's lime-green, **Yolande's** warm brown skin, green eyes, and medium brown hair shine.

With her peachy-brown skin, warm brown eyes, and medium brown hair, **Edda** is a bright Spring with a smile and dimples to make the birds sing.

A Spring woman can be flamboyant and extravagant. She has so many bright and exciting colors in her palette that she is always blooming. With her, all things seem possible.

The Spring Palette

The Spring palette includes both warm neutrals and warm bright colors. Use your neutrals for business and the others for nonbusiness clothing and accessories. For more about wardrobe building with your colors see page 84.

Warm and Cool

Cool: *Anita*

The key to the seasonal color theory is contained in the words *warm* and *cool*.

Winters and Summers are the cool ones with blue, rose, and purple undertones to their skins. Anita is a cool Winter. See how wonderful she looks in Winter's red. Her skin is rosy brown and translucent, her hair and eyes are deep and sensous.

But put her in Prerana's olive, and Anita would look muddy and tired. She needs the cool colors to reflect her natural beauty.

Warm: *Prerana*

Autumns and Springs are the warm women of color with golden undertones.

Prerana's golden skin and warm brown eyes and hair look rich and luxuriant in her muted olive sweater and bright gold necklace and earrings.

This warm olive green and gold enhance the warmth of Prerana's coloring. In contrast, cool emerald green would make her look sallow.

Text continues from page 32

Phase One: Your Color Life-style

Open your closet door. Pull out the pieces that you wear most and for which you receive the most compliments. Arrange them by color on a rack outside your closet where the light is most natural. Now look back in your closet at the hodgepodge of other colors—the ones you seldom wear and for which you get the fewest compliments. These are the colors you are wearing when your co-workers ask if you are sick or tired. Leave them in the closet and shut the door.

You won't miss them or be tempted to wear them. I had a lot of colors in my closet that were great, but each time I wore that olive green dress, for instance, I would feel depressed—and be treated by my friends as if I were—until I took it off.

Now look at your clothing colors and at the groupings of colors that follow. (You can see these colors on pages 34 and 35.) Which group of colors best reflects the dominant colors in your wardrobe?

Cool		Warm	
WINTER	SUMMER	AUTUMN	SPRING
Black	Flannel gray	Dark brown	Warm beige
Sapphire blue	Baby blue	Teal	Turquoise
Clear red	Rose	Orange	Shrimp
Emerald green	Apple green	Olive green	Lime
Deep yellow	Light yellow	Gold	Bright yellow

Now, list the wardrobe pieces on your rack by color. *Save this chart.* It is the beginning of your total new look.

	Wardrobe Piece	Color
1.	_____	_____
2.	_____	_____
3.	_____	_____
4.	_____	_____
5.	_____	_____
6.	_____	_____
7.	_____	_____
8.	_____	_____
9.	_____	_____
10.	_____	_____

Phase Two: The Skin Test

1. Remove all makeup and tinted contacts.

2. If you've colored your hair, cover it with clear plastic. Otherwise, do not cover it.

3. Position yourself in front of a mirror where there is natural sunlight. Look closely at your hair, skin, and eyes.

Your Hair. Before reading further, *really* examine your hair. Try to describe it, taking note of details such as highlights (how the sun brings out lighter or brighter coloring), depth of color (how deep the brown or auburn is), and the signs of graying.

Your Skin. What do you see? Is your skin clear in coloring? Is there natural cheek color? Are the lip and eye areas pronounced? Describe the colors you think you see beneath your skin; these are the natural colors that we will use makeup to enhance.

The color of your skin comes from pigmentation. There are three pigments: melanin (brown), carotene (yellow), and hemoglobin (red). It is the combination of these three pigments that gives you your unique skin color.

Summer and Winter have blue, rose, and purple undertones, while Autumn and Spring have yellow and golden undertones. For some of you, the skin tone will be very easy to determine, but for others you'll recognize that you have a more subtle skin tone that requires a little study. Your skin may be tanned or not evenly colored. In these cases, compare the skin behind the ears and at the nape of the neck and the insides of your wrists to determine the exact skin coloring. These areas are covered more often, so their skin tone is usually true and even.

Your Eyes. Last, look closely at your eyes. Describe them; think in terms of the iris but also the rings of color around the iris. Look for a tendency for the eyes to change or reflect color.

Now look at the following descriptions of each of the four seasons. You should be able to find your skin, hair, and eye color in the one season that describes you best:

Winter

Skin:
- ☐ White with pink tone
- ☐ Rose beige
- ☐ Olive
- ☐ Black (blue undertone)
- ☐ Black (purple undertone)
- ☐ Pearl white

Hair:
- ☐ Silver gray
- ☐ Darkest brown
- ☐ Darkest brown with red highlights
- ☐ Black (blue tone)

Eyes:
- ☐ Black
- ☐ Darkest brown
- ☐ Hazel (gray tone, green, or blue)
- ☐ Dark blue
- ☐ Gray green

Winter Characteristics

Note: Native American and African-American Winters have skin that is cool in appearance and their eyes are usually deep-set.

Hair: Most Winters have black to dark-brown hair, but it can range from light brown to darkest brown, sometimes with red highlights. Black hair that becomes salt-and-pepper then silver gray or pure white is also typical of a Winter woman. Winters are more likely to gray prematurely. It is rare to find a Winter who is a redhead or a blonde.

Skin: If you are Winter, you will notice blue or pink/rose undertones in your skin. Don't expect these subtle undertones to pop out at you. Olive-skinned people, for instance, can be Winters, too. This olive-toned skin may appear to be golden, but the undertones are really more blue-green than yellow. Stay away from brown-based colors, which make the skin look muddy. Winters can omit blush because they have naturally pink or blue undertones and dark alluring eyes.

Eyes: Winter women have very deep eye color—warm brown, black, or hazel (a combination of gray-brown and blue or green).

Summer

Skin:
- ☐ Beige
- ☐ Beige/pink
- ☐ Light olive
- ☐ White translucent
- ☐ Light skin: pale beige

Hair:
- ☐ Dark blond
- ☐ Light ash brown
- ☐ Silver
- ☐ Brunette

Eyes:
- ☐ Brown
- ☐ Blue
- ☐ Gray blue
- ☐ Cool blue
- ☐ Green mixed with brown

Summer Characteristics

Note: African-American and Hispanic Summers have dark beige/ pink and rosy skin; Asian Summers have pale beige, ivory, or light olive skin with pink blushes.

Hair: Summers often have light-brown to blond hair as children. As they mature, their hair darkens to light ash brown or ash blond. Summer women of color usually turn brunette.

Skin: Most Summer women have pinkish skin or a little pink color in the cheek area. Hispanic and African-American Summer women have dark beige/pink or rosy skin, while Asian Summers have pale beige, ivory, or very light olive skin tones. Their skin is often translucent.

Eyes: Summer features are soft, so these women look youthful for much of their lives. Summer eyes are often cool blue or gray blue, softest brown, or even green mixed with brown.

Autumn

Skin:
☐ Ivory

☐ Peach

☐ Golden beige

☐ Brown

Hair:
☐ Dark brown

☐ Black brown

☐ Dark blond

☐ Copper brown

☐ Auburn

☐ Red

Eyes:
☐ Brown

☐ Golden brown

☐ Green

☐ Hazel

Autumn Characteristics

Note: Most Autumn Hispanics and Asians have peachy or warm brown skin, but they may have ruddy skin with bright red cheeks. African-American and other Autumn women of color are more golden with warm beige or warm deep brown skin tones. Autumns are *never* olive-toned.

Hair: The Autumn woman of color has reddish hair with golden highlights. Her hair may resemble Summer's light ash brown or dark blond, but there are more golden tones—light golden brown, chestnut, copper-brown, strawberry, or auburn. Autumns with black hair are extremely rare. During my career, I've encountered a number of Autumns who have dyed their hair from light brown to black. Unfortunately, this changes the clarity of their skin and makes it particularly difficult to discover their true season.

Skin: Autumn skin is ivory, peach, golden beige, or brown, and may appear golden. Autumns have little color in their cheeks, so blushes make them more glamorous.

Eyes: Autumn eyes are usually warm brown, green, or blue. Blue-eyed Autumns usually have golden or brown flecks in the iris that make their eyes look steel-blue from a distance.

Spring

Skin:
- ☐ Ivory
- ☐ Peach
- ☐ Gold/beige
- ☐ Brown
- ☐ Light golden brown

Hair:
- ☐ Medium brown
- ☐ Dark brown
- ☐ Blond/gold
- ☐ Golden brown
- ☐ Strawberry blond

Eyes:
- ☐ Light brown
- ☐ Amber brown
- ☐ Blue
- ☐ Green

Spring Characteristics

Note: African-American and Hispanic Springs are light and golden with a clear bright look, and Asian Springs have very light to ivory skin.

Hair: Most Springs have golden blond, medium-light red, or golden to medium-brown hair. Some Spring women have bright, clear, natural blond hair. Others have medium to dark brown hair with or without red highlights.

Skin: Spring skin tones are ivory, peach, golden beige, or brown. African-American and Hispanic Springs are light and golden with a lot of clarity. Asian Springs have very light to ivory skin. Springs can do without blush because of the natural warmth around their foreheads and cheeks.

Eyes: Spring eyes are clear, light to amber brown, or blue or green with yellow flecks.

Tie-Breaker Questions

If you are *still* having trouble determining your season, answer the following questions.

1. Do I look my best in black, pure white, or red? Do others compliment me when I am wearing these colors? (If you answered yes, then you are undoubtedly a Winter.)

2. Do I radiate in pastels like sea blue and mint green, or am I better in beige and lime? (If you answered sea blue and mint green, you are a Summer. Better in beige and lime, you are a Spring.)

3. Am I striking in a black blazer with a bright white blouse or in a dark brown blazer with a beige blouse? (If brown is better on you than black and if black makes you look tired, you are an Autumn. Whatever your season, if black makes you look tired, you are *not* a Winter.)

4. Am I exciting in golden brown and red-orange or rosy brown with dusty rose? (You are an Autumn if you vibrate in golden brown and red-orange; if your response was rosy brown and dusty rose, you are a Summer.)

Now you know your Season. This means you are a true woman of color.

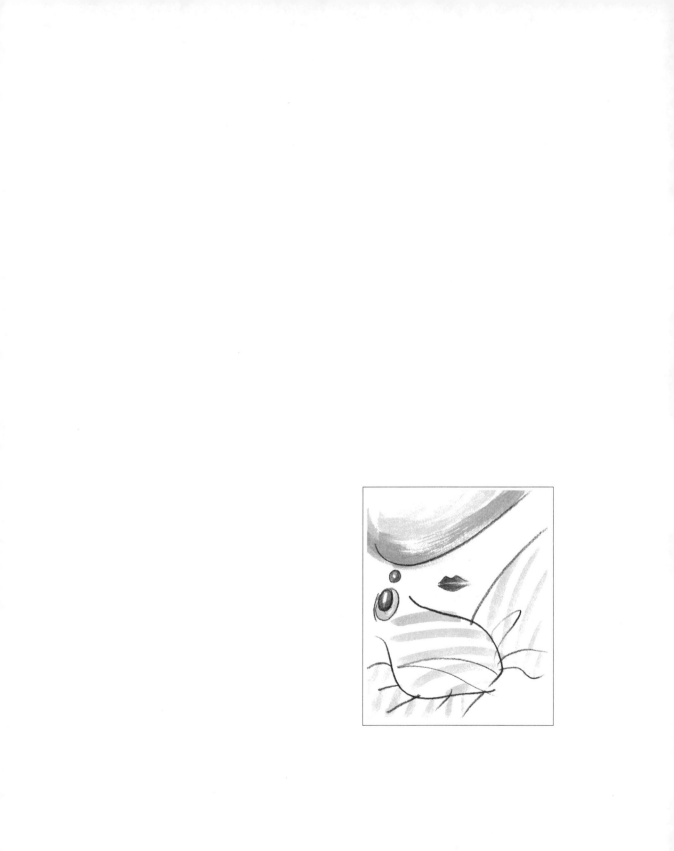

CHAPTER 2

Your Color Personality

Your appearance *can* influence the development of your personality. If you're a Winter, with rich blue-black skin and sparkling black eyes and hair, your looks are vivid and dramatic. And I'll bet you are, too. On the other hand, if you have light brown hair, pink cheeks, and wide hazel eyes, your looks are dreamy and romantic. And I'll bet you are, too. *See what I mean?*

You can conduct a test of your own. As you go about your day, take a mental note of all the women you come in contact with who have distinctively dark features. I'll bet you will find similarities in professions as well as similarities in their style of dress.

Many times you've probably responded to a situation, an article of clothing, or the actions of others with the expression, "That's just not me!" What you are expressing here is your *personality*—the quality of being a person, an individual. It is this distinction that makes you YOU, and no one else. Your very personal identity is your personality and is what makes you know you are different from the next person.

How Your Appearance Can Influence Your Personality

Yes, it's your personality that tells you in a matter of seconds who you are and what is or is not an expression of you. And so it is with determining the colors that are you. Most people see color in very generalized ways, but subconsciously they attach meaning to various colors. So let me help you learn to use color as an element of expression, as artists do to symbolize something that is cultural or traditional, to create mood and emotion, and to identify an object. This way, when you choose colors, you'll think of yourself as an artist who is creating a work that is expressive of your personality.

A little adaptation of vocabulary is needed in order to avoid generalizations about color and beauty. *Hues* are the names by which we identify colors: red, yellow, green, blue, and violet are examples. *Color* is light. It is made up of differing wave lengths of light. *Tone* is its value or quality, as in whether it is deep or light, muted or bright, warm or cool.

Let's not confuse color and skin tone. For instance, when using blue to describe skin tone, we think of very dark skin. But as you saw in the previous chapter, this assumption is not necessarily true. Five different women of color can have blue as an underlying skin tone, but their skin color can vary from very light to dark. The reason for this phenomenon is that a woman's overall tone is affected by color in the skin *as well as* the colors she is wearing. An energetic and sparkling Spring woman, for instance, is as capricious as nature, and often as delicate as her season. The colors of her palette—yellow, lime green, and sea blue—are as light, bright, and whimsical as her personality.

A dramatic Winter, tall and imposing, demands attention, a prime position on stage. Even if her stature is not large, her climatic coloring of clear, primary colors commands attention.

Gentle Summer, as soft as the breeze through the leaves, is frequently the quiet one between capricious Spring and vigorous Autumn. Summers are nurturing and restful people, anxious to please. They glisten in muted cool colors.

Earthy Autumn wears the heavy, warm tones of her palette with the vigor of her golden harvest season. She is a woman who gives limitless amounts of energy to her career. When she is daring and wears her own particular shade of red-orange, her confidence soars and there is no stopping her!

This chapter will reveal your personality by both the colors you choose and the colors that your heritage gave you, and will help you see yourself through the spectrum of the four seasons.

Winter Women of Color—Cooooool

Winter is the season of mixed emotions. It brings with it the holidays we enjoy and the hibernation from the cold. Its roaring fires bring us close to the hearths of home, whether in our memories or in person. Here we gather inner strength for the changes we resolve to make in the new year, and it's here we find the courage to face the next season. Winter is a time of change, the most extreme season between autumn and spring, and a time to celebrate giving.

Winter women have intensity of coloring—the pure whites, blacks, deep reds, and blues that symbolize the season in our mind's eye. Their hair is medium to dark, and their eye color is deep and intense and often exotic with gray and green tones. Winter skin is either very light or very dark, either olive or gray-beige, either pink-beige or blue-black.

A few Winter African Americans, Native Americans, and Asians have pink coloring around the cheek and forehead areas. Age plays a very important role for Winters, adding distinction to their looks. But whatever their age, Winters always have vivid coloring.

Because of Winters' color personality, they are dramatic. You'll find them as sales and marketing people, waitresses and restaurant owners, beauty consultants, television personalities, politicians, actresses—a whole host of energetic careers that put them before an audience. They can be lawyers, teachers, or writers, but often they'll be trial lawyers, and fiery inner-city principals, and commercial fiction writers. Oprah Winfrey, Lena Horne, and Connie Chung, for example, are Winters. They have deep, intense skin and eye coloring. They are forthright and dramatic and can mesmerize their audiences. And, because Winters are dramatic, their strongest colors are black, royal purple, clear red, and pure white.

One of my favorite clients is Grace, an African-American lawyer in Washington, D.C. She began her law career eleven years ago and is now a partner in her firm. She is a trial lawyer and her dramatic Winter personality is an asset as she appeals to judges and juries. Grace has the cool skin tone of Winter. Her complexion is light but her features are dark and dramatic. She exhibits a strong presence even in the way she walks and moves. We know that she is on her way to some place very important, and that when she arrives there, she will make a striking impression.

Summer Women of Color—Soft Cool Breezes

Ah, summer! The season we associate with relaxation, dreaming, resting, and giving way to our fantasies. It's the season to wear less, and, yes, it's the season to shed (clothes, weight, life's burdens) and to wiggle our toes and relax. It is truly the season of liberation.

Most Summers possess a lot of clarity. *Clarity* is the characteristic that gives their skin translucence. No matter the age of a Summer, she is usually young in appearance with soft brown hair and skin that defies age.

Darker Summers can have purplish-red highlights in their hair. Their eyes are most often cool-blue, gray-blue, or gentle black. Compared with Winters, they are altogether softer, dreamier, more flexible, and less formal women who prefer a casual but sophisticated look. The Summer woman does not restrict herself. She wants to be able to change with her moods when wearing her strongest colors of charcoal, navy, and deep rose.

Because of their soft hearts and fluid personalities, Summers make good doctors and nurses, homemakers, editors, public relations specialists, social activists, beauty consultants, writers, artists, and classroom teachers. Japanese Princess Masako Owada and Jonetta Cole, president of Spelman (one of the country's leading historically black colleges) are Summers.

So is my dear friend Lia. She is a woman of Latin heritage who has a cool, rosy complexion, blue-gray eyes, and white hair with a touch of black woven neatly throughout. Her skin is youthful and pure. She is the greatest homemaker and mother I've ever known. I gave Lia a color analysis about three years ago, and the soft, cool colors of her palette are just right for the youthful, no-frills look she prefers. Her favorite clothes are sportswear, which she wears often because she is an avid boater.

Myra is one of my African-American clients I most admire because of her chosen profession. A gentle Summer with light brown skin, soft brown hair, and gray eyes, she is typical of the nurturing personality of her season. Myra teaches our children, and so, in my book, is responsible for the future of our world. She recognizes that as a teacher she is a role model and the center of attention in the classroom for long hours every day. In developing her wardrobe, we paid close attention to making a fashion statement that was both appropriate and creative; we used the cool colors of her palette. For Myra, it is important to make a statement that reflects her leadership role and to exhibit a style she would like her students to emulate.

Autumn Women of Color—Warm and Earthy

A harvest moon, the bright hues of change, and a sense of abundance—all make autumn a special season. With autumn comes a need to get back to business, to produce. With autumn comes renewed vigor after the heat and the need to prepare for winter. In autumn, we are ready to abandon the capriciousness of summer and to get serious.

The Autumn woman is earthy and sensuous. Her hair may be dark blond or dark brown and is characterized by red or gold highlights. Her skin tone is usually peach, ivory, golden, beige, or brown. With her golden skin tone, she can wear olive green, orange, and deep brown with authority and brilliance. In these colors gentle Summers and sparkling Springs would be faded flowers, while Winters would turn puce and lose their drama.

Autumn women are sophisticated and seldom seen as naive. Acutely aware of her surroundings, an Autumn makes a strong impact on those around her. She wears browns and orange-red better than any other season, using browns to accentuate her strength and orange-reds for additional flair to reflect her vigor and energy. Extremely adept in the business world, she can wear an ivory blouse under a brown jacket for the more refined, sophisticated look. The Autumn woman is often the person who closes the deal, anchors the evening news with color and excitement, or provides the needed psychological therapy for patients who find her both knowledgeable and strong. Vanessa Williams, Gloria Estefan, Janet Jackson, and Carol Moseley-Braun are strong Autumns.

Karen is an Autumn from the Bahamas. She is responsible for 3,500 employees at Resorts International. She wears strong Autumn colors—deep browns, orange-reds, and darkest navy—to enhance her corporate power and authority. Her colors are especially important when she has to meet with the president of the corporation. She looks striking and important in her orange-red gabardine shirt waist dress, brown shoes, and gold accessories.

Doris is a true Autumn. Her hair is dark golden brown and enhances her rich skin color, which she inherited from her German mother and African-American father. She is a media consultant and needs to be dressed for the occasion at all times. Her favorite color from the Autumn palette is olive green, which she often sports in a tweed suit with a beige or cream blouse. Doris loves to experiment with shoes and accessories. She knows that the colors she wears must hold the attention of her audience.

Denise is one of those clients who makes it all worth the effort. She is an African-American with blue-black skin. We began the creation of an overall image for her almost five years ago, and her active professional life made her the perfect client for developing a total image. When Denise and I met, she was the president of a division of the National Bar Association. She attended political, professional, and social events from sunup to sundown and, in between, could be found on the television news as a spokesperson for her organization.

After identifying her seasonal palette as Winter, we began organizing Denise's wardrobe and makeup and purchasing the colors that were right for her. Organization was the key because the day was often not long enough to accommodate even a quick change. Her daily schedule meant we had to provide sophistication through a hairstyle, clothing, and accessories that were also quick and easy to achieve. Soon, Denise was at ease with a total look that worked for a day in which she appeared in court in the morning, attended a bar association meeting in the afternoon, and made a striking entrance at a reception in the evening.

Spring Women of Color—Warm and Bright

Spring is the season we associate with renaissance—rebirth. It is the season in which all things seem possible. As the flowers bloom, so do Spring women.

Most Spring women possess bright coloring with golden or strawberry blond, light red, or golden brown hair. Some have medium to dark brown hair without red highlights, although it is more unusual. Still, their skin is golden and their eyes are warm brown, clear green, or blue with yellow flecks. They have clarity and contrast in their coloring.

The majority of Springs have ivory, peach, golden beige, or golden brown skin tones. African-American Springs are medium to light and golden with a clear appearance. Asian Springs, while possessing dark hair, have very delicate pearl to ivory skin tones.

A Spring woman is usually flamboyant and extravagant. She has so many bright and exciting colors in her palette that she must take care not to overdo in her best colors of caramel, turquoise, shrimp, and sunshine yellow.

Spring women are successful business women, performers, politicians, architects, graphic artists, athletes, and all sorts of creative professionals, just like the other seasons. But they tend toward drama and high energy, like their Winter cousins, and appreciate an audience. Springs are more delicate in appearance than Winters and less strident in their presentation, but they overflow with creative ideas and energy. Washington's Mayor Sharon Pratt Kelly is a vivid Spring with a true Spring woman's energy. Yolande Donaldson, wife of the Bahamian ambassador, is an energetic Spring who is dedicated to women's health issues. Each of these women has personality and style, as well as great charm when entertaining audiences.

Joyce is one of my most interesting African-American Spring clients. When she reached forty, she made some realistic decisions about her appearance and health. She recognized the importance of healthy living and shed the limitations of what she calls the "magazine image." She is a vivacious advertising and marketing executive who is taller than most Springs and who has learned, with my help, to be comfortable in a size twelve. Now she knows how to shop for her well-proportioned body.

Joyce began to gray early, during her late twenties, and when she came to me, she was eager to color her hair. I recommended a sun-kissed brown hair color that is consistent with her Spring palette. Now she sports a no-fuss and sophisticated hair cut that is both manageable and flattering. Because she enjoys spending a lot of time outdoors, Joyce's wardrobe includes casual but sophisticated pants, vests, and blazers. One day, she will be very comfortable at the country home or horse farm she wants to own.

Let's move on to the next chapter and find out how to put professional wardrobes together so you'll have flexibility when you dress in the morning, no matter what your exciting day might bring. Colors, makeup, and wardrobe are the most important ingredients of this new, more empowered you.

CHAPTER 3

Color Your Career

It is unlikely that many Americans were prepared for the impact of their new First Lady, Hillary Rodham Clinton. For the longest time women in this country, and others, were reared to "stand in the shadow" of their famous and/or successful husbands. They were to be patient and supportive and do only things that enhanced *his* career. Well, this First Lady, and a lot of others from this generation on down, will break the chains that bind. This First Lady is one we all want to emulate. She stands *next* to her best friend and husband.

Mrs. Clinton has set a precedent for First Ladies and a role model for women who are married to men in public office. She has even beaten the odds in parenting. Chelsea seems to be a happy, thriving child whose father spends as much time with her as her mother does. Mrs. Clinton is highly respected for her intellectual abilities, and she is one of the only First Ladies given visible and substantive assignments by the President.

As her husband took the oath of office, some people in this country responded to her forceful presence with concern. Who is going to be running the country anyway: Clinton or Rodham Clinton? As the inaugural activities waned and the first 100 days passed, even the First Lady's appearance became an issue. Now Hillary Rodham Clinton has found her niche and her fashion statement. We've watched her test several image consultants with new hair and clothing styles. She has developed a look that is polished and very professional. She looks like a world leader—but she's done so without sacrificing femininity. Her looks say that she is strong, knowledgeable, and confident. I salute her.

It's Our Time to Move Up the Career Ladder

Historically, women were told that "pretty is as pretty does." But we all know that how you look makes a big difference in how you are treated on the job and at home. Perversely, we've also been taught that "image" is a frivolous word. But as women work to reach up and break through the glass ceilings, we have become increasingly aware that our image conveys a message even before we begin to speak or before our resume of distinguished credentials is considered. Women have had to fight for the right to vote and for equal pay. Too often, we have had to listen while our causes and gender were demeaned. And we're still fighting, especially we women of color. But times are changing.

We women of color are moving up the career ladder faster than ever. The gender-neutral adage that the medium is the message is still viable. As more opportunities for women become available and we begin to direct our attention to the "whole woman," we must strive to remain at our personal best.

Developing a Style Appropriate to Your Job

So you've earned your credentials—a certificate of training, a bachelor's degree, even your M.B.A. or Ph.D.; now, you need an individual style to get you through the doors to your dream job. Well, follow me through the next pages. You are going to achieve an awareness of your total image—from an analysis of your color palette to your makeup and hair, and a "professionalized" wardrobe that will help you march right up that career ladder.

Self-confidence is key in defining your style. When you look good, you feel good. Imagine someone giving an important speech in front of hundreds of people. She begins to comb through her hair with her fingers, checks her scarf, buttons and unbuttons her jacket, and then buttons it again. Tell me what your impression might be. Her nervous behavior tells me she is not confident about either her appearance or her message. As a result, she does not convey her message convincingly to the audience. No matter how long she has prepared for this moment, her message is lost—and so are her potential clients and business profits.

First impressions are *lasting* impressions. People tend to listen to what their eyes tell them. When you are introduced to new people, they usually make a decision about you within the first five seconds. That five-second look is based on the colors you are wearing closest to your face, your hairstyle, and, of course, your body language.

Dressing for Confidence

Dressing for confidence gives women a chance to focus on their ideas and goals. We've talked about color analysis, and you know what your season is. Now that you have narrowed down what colors and styles are just for you, you will begin to experience a sense of confidence that frees your mind to cope with the details of your career. You are able to deal with the issues at hand and later reap the benefits.

While most of us don't land executive-level jobs with America's Fortune 500 companies, it is interesting to note that many companies offer, as a part of their executive perks, image and wardrobe enhancement stipends. These big corporations know that the way their management looks can be the first important sign of how their products are received in the marketplace.

Can you judge a book by its cover? In the 1980s if you were observant enough, you could ride public transportation and identify the lawyers, professors, doctors, and other professionals simply by the way they were dressed. "Dress correctness" for women was the "navy tailored-suit look" of male corporate America. Today, dress codes are not quite as defined.

But trendy can be risky. The flip side is also true: so can an outdated or dull appearance. Professional style combines good taste with your own personality, allowing your looks to complement but not detract from the message you are imparting. When you identify your niche, you can develop your style—always comfortable but appropriate for the work you do.

A Television Anchor Who Loves Color

My friend and client, Pat, for instance, was analyzed as a Winter by another color consultant. Pat, a very charming and beautiful African-American woman, is a weekend news anchor for a television station in a major market. She is very petite and felt overwhelmed by the heavy Winter colors that had been assigned to her. She liked some of the colors, but others she did not.

I analyzed Pat and did a color "add." I found she is a Summer with Winter add-ons. What that meant to Pat was that she could continue to wear some of the strong colors of Winter *only* if she wore her icy pastels in pinks, blues, and greens to enhance her dominant colors of black, purple, fuchsia, and sapphire blue. For example, a fuchsia suit with an icy pink silk blouse or a deep purple suit with an icy blue blouse were beautiful on her. Pat loves colors and so she is able to wear a multitude of cool colors, enhancing her personality to the fullest. She has a lot of energy and is a great communicator. We want to be sure her audiences enjoy *watching* her on television as much as they enjoy listening to her.

"Dress Correctness" with Flair

Washington, D.C., where I live and work, is still a town of "dress correctness." According to the Bureau of Labor Statistics, a higher percentage of women are employed (65 percent) than the national average (54 percent). In Washington women have taken a fairly conservative route in dressing for success, but they have adopted a dress style with lots of flair, using long lines in blazers, short skirts, mid-length skirts with lots of pleats, wide leg slacks, and vests with contrasting colors to blend with the total look. The look is not at all like the Washington man's traditional work attire, which also could be called the professional's uniform.

I gave an image presentation to a group of working women recently; it was extraordinary to watch these accomplished women examine their own natural beauty with the same intensity they had applied to reaching their career goals. They had worked hard and had not found the time to examine their own best looks in their struggle to succeed.

So let's look at one of the women in this group. Betty, an attractive African-American woman, is very articulate and has a charming personality. She coordinated her clothing well, but she was wearing all of the wrong colors—at least those that were closest to her face. She was wearing lots of blues and blacks and accenting everything with white, which made her skin ashy.

We had a color analysis session and noted her warm natural colors. She's an Autumn. She's about five feet six inches, wears a size ten, and has strong features with natural warm brown eyes and hair with natural golden highlights. Betty reminds you of Whitney Houston, but because of her profession, we had to keep in mind that too much makeup and such bold accessories wouldn't be appropriate on her. For Betty is the first woman to serve as chief of an agency where men had always held her position. So we chose power colors—blacks, browns and orange-reds—for her blazers, skirts, slacks, shoes, and coats. We used softer colors for accessories—oyster, maize, and sage, all of which are in the Autumn family. Her jewelry is gold and her pearls are cream. I changed her makeup to a warm base and lipsticks from red to orange-red.

I have continued to meet Betty at social and business functions and she is self-confident, knowing that she looks as much of a leader as she is.

A Little Bit of Black in Every Palette

Tara, on the other hand, is a lawyer in private practice. When I met her, I knew immediately she was a Summer. Her mother is Asian and her father is African-American. Almost everything she wore was black—too heavy and overpowering for her more delicate coloring. I gave her a color analysis and immediately she could identify with all of the colors in her palette. She loved the navy, midnight blue, and rose brown, but was disappointed that she shouldn't wear jet black.

Since Tara and many other women of other seasons expressed displeasure without black in their palettes, I discussed the situation with Carole Jackson. We both thought adding black to all the palettes would make a lot of beautiful women very happy. So we did—with the strictest understanding that black should *not* be worn close to the face. When black is worn near Autumn and Spring faces, the result is a hard or tired look. So Autumn can wear black but must contrast it with beige, for example, or peach next to the face. Summers can wear black, but must put pink or powder blue next to their faces. Blouses and scarves serve this purpose well. Spring can wear a black skirt and blazer, but should put a shrimp or coral blouse and gold jewelry near her face.

Now Tara is a happy Summer, and we have expanded her basic black with blues and pinks and some off-whites with silver accessories, making her blacks the accent pieces.

Improve Your Job by Improving Your Looks

Many of my other clients have improved their jobs when they improved their looks. For instance, Kiko, who is Japanese, has lots of energy—what we might call a type-A personality. Because she travels a great deal for her job, Kiko's ability to concentrate on the work at hand was hampered by her worry about what to pack and how her clothes would look after a long plane trip. An added concern was that she had tons of accessories but no basics. We added some to her wardrobe, selecting fabrics that would not wrinkle in an attempt to alleviate her fears. Gabardines, silk with polyester, and crepes were perfect for her. These fabrics are a little more expensive, but if you invest in conservative lines and hem lengths, you'll have these pieces for years to come.

We began by purchasing one blazer, one mid-length and one knee-length skirt, an oversized polyester sweater blazer, one turtleneck top, two open-collar blouses of silk polyester (one neutral color and one colored), and one pair of slacks. Today Kiko is ready to travel with her mind focused on her work, and she sees the positive results of wardrobe preparation.

Make Your Uniform an Elegant One

If an elegant uniform happens to be your company's dress code, color can help you create a little individuality.

Julie works for a major hotel chain that requires her to wear a uniform. She came to me for a color analysis to use for her personal wardrobe and discovered that she can use the accessory and makeup information for her day-to-day dressing routine. A beautiful woman of Vietnamese and Caucasian heritage, she is a Summer and should wear white pearl studs instead of the cream pearl jewelry she had been wearing. Julie stopped trying to wear Spring makeup colors with her Spring green uniform, and I showed her how she could wear her Summer makeup with whatever she wore. It made dressing so much easier and took the tedium and time out of makeup selection.

After Julie became a believer in the Women of Color theory, she convinced her boss to have the entire staff take my training. Soon all the staff members began to look better and feel better about themselves and their positions. A letter from the CEO of the company thanked me for the work that I had done with his staff: "They have become customer-service oriented. They smile a lot more. So thank you."

Text continues on page 89

BUSINESS BASICS:

Colors for Your Career

Every woman needs authority on the job, and a carefully built professional wardrobe can help you achieve the look that says you mean what you say and you know what you're talking about. Use an Authority Color from your palette to begin your 1 + 1 Professional Wardrobe. Start with a two-piece suit, a skirt, slacks, and blazer in your Authority Color to give you the sophisticated look of the professional. Add another color in your palette or a pattern with both colors for sweaters, turtlenecks, and blouses. Every season can wear black, but if you aren't a Winter, don't wear it close to your face. Winters can wear dark navy with style and so can Summers. But Summers are better in flannel gray, Autumns in aubergine or dark brown, and Springs in taupe or warm medium brown.

Authority Colors

Winters: black, dark navy

Summers: navy, flannel gray

Autumns: aubergine, dark brown

Springs: taupe, warm medium brown

Addis

Addis, an Ethiopian Winter, is shown here in a clear red blouse in the second color of her 1+1 Professional Wardrobe. Note how her elegant silver jewelry complement her dark hair and eyes and pull her business look together.

Jewelry and the Seasons

Jewelry should add glamour and style and balance to your fashion statement. It should be your most important accessory investment. **Dramatic Winters** need bold, modern, one-of-a-kind jewelry in silver or crystal. Their pearls should be white, and their colored stones black, midnight blue, emerald or ruby red. **Classic Summers** prefer white or pink pearls, understated watches, and small earrings in silver, pearl, soft gray, blue, or pink to match their necklaces. **Warm, earthy Autumns** like large ethnic or high fashion jewelry in gold, bronze, or copper. Amethysts, turquoise, and fire opals are their colored stones. **Sporty Springs** are not jewelry lovers, but simple off-white pearls, a gold watch, and small earrings will complement their look. If they want to be more adventurous, their jewelry should be simple with small colored stones from their palette.

Winter: Colors for Your Wardrobe

The Winter Woman builds her wardrobe around her intense and dramatic personality. Whether it's career, leisure, or evening attire, she strives to bring a sense of drama to her wardrobe selection. Her color palette has deep, rich, clear colors: deep blues, reds, black, and white.

These clear, cool hues are found in the fabrics of designers Donna Karan and Ellen Tracy. Donna Karan's navy blues, grays, and blacks are suited to the Winter woman. The whites, reds, and purples of Ellen Tracy emphasize Winter's fire and ice. "Frosty" and "icy" are the adjectives that describe her colors.

The Winter woman is drawn to the metallic silver and platinum colors that only she can wear well. The Winter palette *excludes* milky browns, russets, and oranges. They are *not* the colors for Winter.

Winter 1 + 1 Wardrobe Combinations

Start with color! It's the only way to begin building your wardrobe. Here are some of the color combinations that are great for creating the outfits of the many roles the Winter woman plays. Use the Classic and Neutral combinations to create the sophisticated business woman or author. Softer and Romantic combinations bring out the alluring and demure look for a special Winter evening. The Natural and Earthy combinations give even the most casual outfit a sophisticated elegance.

For your 1+1 Professional Wardrobe, remember to start with an Authority Color. For Winters that will be black or midnight blue. When you reach the pinnacle of your career, be brave and start a new 1 + 1 in clear red. But you really need authority to wear this color with verve.

Winter Characteristics
- ❏ Deep, intense eye color
- ❏ Deep hair colors of black to dark brown
- ❏ Stunning in contrasting, deep colors
- ❏ Looks best in strong, clear colors
- ❏ Pure whites, blacks, and deep reds complement her looks

Winter's Dislikes
- ❏ Avoids olives and pumpkins
- ❏ Avoids earth tones for clothing
- ❏ Avoids outfits of all fragile floral pastels
- ❏ Often says tan is her least favorite color

A Wardrobe that Promotes the Right Image...and Grows with Your Career

Here are the twelve basic pieces to purchase when your career is beginning and your salary is small. Plan these twelve basic pieces around one of Winter's Authority Colors, like black or dark navy, plus a color from your palette, like silver or wine. Then build up to the mid-level and top-level wardrobes appropriate to your profession. You can always add another color from your palette as your career and your wardrobe needs grow. But you'll be astounded at how many different outfits you can create from the first 1 + 1 Professional Wardrobe you purchase:

- ❏ One all-weather overcoat with a zip-out lining
- ❏ One blazer
- ❏ One cardigan sweater
- ❏ Two turtlenecks or mock turtleneck tops
- ❏ Two blouses, one with tie
- ❏ One pair of slacks
- ❏ One mid-length skirt
- ❏ One knee-length skirt
- ❏ One over-sized sweater
- ❏ One vest (use Chapter 5 to determine length according to height and weight)

Winter's 1 + 1 Wardrobe Combinations

Classic and Neutral

Black/White Dark Navy/Fuchsia Clear Red/White

Soft and Romantic

Periwinkle/White Black/Silver Wine/Icy Pink

Natural and Earthy

Mauve/Black Slate Forest Green/White Platinum/Taupe

Summer: Colors for Your Wardrobe

The Summer Woman is perhaps the real artist of all the seasons. She brings the assets of flexibility and artistic temperament to the challenge of building her wardrobe. What others may see as a task, she sees as an adventure, and she brainstorms and revamps until she gets it right.

The rich, cooler hues of white, blue, and pink characterize the Summer palette. The cool blues and grays of designer Anne Klein and Ellen Tracy's cooler white blouses are suited to the Summer woman. Soft and muted are the adjectives that describe the colors of Summers.

The Summer palette *excludes* earthy greens, deep browns, and vivid oranges.

Summer's 1 + 1 Wardrobe Combinations

No frills, no confusion! Just give the Summer artist her palette and let her get to it. Here are great color combinations for the Summer woman. For creating the perfect outfit for work in the classroom, hospital, or doctor's office, or even at home, use the Classic and Neutral combinations. Summer's evenings are made more sultry and steamy by the Softer and Romantic combinations. And Summer will know just what to do with the Natural and Earthy combinations because she loves her casual but classic look.

Summer should start a 1 + 1 Professional Wardrobe with her Authority Color of navy or flannel gray, plus another color from her palette. These will give her a look of sophistication in keeping with her soft features and hair color.

Summer Characteristics
- ❏ Cool, gentle eye color
- ❏ Lighter hair colors of dark blonde and ash brown
- ❏ Stunning in complementary hues
- ❏ Looks best in cool hues
- ❏ Rich, cool blues, grays and white accentuate her looks

Summer's Dislikes
- ❏ Avoids yellows and oranges
- ❏ Avoids earth tones for clothing
- ❏ Avoids all semblance of frills and bows
- ❏ Often says avocado is her least favorite color

A Wardrobe that Promotes the Right Image...and Grows with Your Career

Here are the twelve basic pieces to purchase when your career is beginning and your salary is small. Plan these twelve basic pieces around one of Summer's Authority Colors , like navy or flannel gray, plus a color from your palette, like pink or sky blue. Then build up to the mid-level and top-level wardrobes appropriate to your profession. You can always add another color from your palette as your career and your wardrobe needs grow. But you'll be astounded at how many different outfits you can create from the first 1 + 1 Professional Wardrobe you purchase:

- ❏ One all-weather overcoat with a zip-out lining
- ❏ One blazer
- ❏ One cardigan sweater
- ❏ Two turtlenecks or mock turtleneck tops
- ❏ Two blouses, one with tie
- ❏ One pair of slacks
- ❏ One mid-length skirt
- ❏ One knee-length skirt
- ❏ One over-sized sweater
- ❏ One vest (use Chapter 5 to determine length according to height and weight)

Summer's 1 + 1 Wardrobe Combinations

Classic and Neutral

Midnight Blue/Light Blue   Navy/Off White   Flannel Gray/Pink

Soft and Romantic

Deep Purple/Lilac   Sky Blue/Pink   Pink/Rose

Natural and Earthy

Mauve/Light Rose   Blue Gray/Taupe   Plum/Light Gray

Autumn: Colors for Your Wardrobe

The Autumn Woman has a palette to envy, and many try and fail to wear her warm and earthy colors. If she is smart, and most Autumns are, she can build a beautiful wardrobe with color. She can wear browns, orange-reds, and olives better than any other season, and she is the only season who can wear the striking metallic sand, copper, and bronze colors.

The rich fabrics of designer Dana Buchman incorporate the orange-reds, browns, and greens that are made for the Autumn woman. Autumn's warm and earthy hues accentuate her sophisticated and sensuous personality. The Autumn woman is drawn to the earth colors, and she can also wear muted navy blue. If there is a palette that appears to have the richest of every color, it is the Autumn palette. The Autumn palette *excludes* pastels, but Autumn women don't care. When it comes to color, they already have it all.

Autumn's 1 + 1 Wardrobe Combinations

When all the warm and earthy colors are yours, it is fun to build a wardrobe around color. And, of course, fun is the basic idea. The Autumn woman is stunning when she accentuates jade green with coral for a hot date. But for her 1 + 1 Professional Wardrobe, she takes the sophisticated look to new heights when she uses her Authority Color of dark brown with ivory for a business meeting, or aubergine with light warm gray.

Autumn Characteristics
- ❏ Warm, deep eyes
- ❏ Golden to medium light hair color
- ❏ Looks best in warm, earthy colors
- ❏ Warm browns and greens are stunning on her

Autumn's Dislikes
- ❏ Avoids pure whites and black
- ❏ Avoids pastels
- ❏ Avoids too casual a look
- ❏ Often says fuschia is her least favorite color

A Wardrobe that Promotes the Right Image...and Grows with Your Career

Here are the twelve basic pieces to purchase when your career is beginning and your salary is small. Plan these twelve basic pieces around one of Autumn's Authority Colors, like dark brown or aubergine, plus a color from your palette, like cream or peach. Then build up to the mid-level and top-level wardrobes appropriate to your profession. You can always add another color from your palette as your career and your wardrobe needs grow. But you'll be astounded at how many different outfits you can create from the first 1 + 1 Professional Wardrobe you purchase:

- ❏ One all-weather overcoat with a zip-out lining
- ❏ One blazer
- ❏ One cardigan sweater
- ❏ Two turtlenecks or mock turtleneck tops
- ❏ Two blouses, one with tie
- ❏ One pair of slacks
- ❏ One mid-length skirt
- ❏ One knee-length skirt
- ❏ One over-sized sweater
- ❏ One vest (use Chapter 5 to determine length according to height and weight)

Autumn's 1 + 1 Wardrobe Combinations

Classic and Neutral
Dark Brown/Ivory   Aubergine/Warm Gray   Teal/Cream

Soft and Romantic
Cream/Pumpkin   Deep Coral/Cream   Peach/Medium Forest

Natural and Earthy
Jade Green/Sage   Taupe/Warm Gray   Khaki/Beige

Spring: Colors for Your Wardrobe

The Spring Woman is flamboyant and loves to wield her palette of bright and exciting colors. Creative and energetic, this woman marshals her colors to create a wardrobe for work or play.

Spring's palette should be seen as a bouquet because every bright hue associated with a flower garden can be found there. Warm, bright yellows, corals, greens, and browns are the preferred hues. The Spring woman can depend on the colors of designer Liz Claiborne for bright greens and corals.

The Spring woman's palette can be called warm and energetic but silky in hue. Only she can wear cognac and colors that are sun-kissed. The Spring palette *excludes* blacks, blue grays, and pure whites.

Spring's 1 + 1 Wardrobe Combinations

The Spring woman finds it is easy to work with color. Because she enjoys the outdoors, she is at ease with the bright colors of her palette. Her flamboyant personality helps her to use these colors extravagantly, and she enjoys it completely.

For her 1 + 1 Professional Wardrobe, she should start with Authority Colors like taupe or bright navy, and add a light bright second color to her twelve basic pieces of clothing.

Spring Characteristics
❏ Clear, deep eyes
❏ Hair colors vary from medium brown to strawberry blonde
❏ Stunning in contrasting colors
❏ Looks best in bright colors
❏ Bright variations on rich browns and corals accentuate her looks

Spring's Dislikes
❏ Avoids black and charcoal gray
❏ Avoids fads and trendy styles
❏ Avoids tight-fitting clothing
❏ Often says purple is her least favorite color

A Wardrobe that Promotes the Right Image...and Grows with Your Career

Here are the twelve basic pieces to purchase when your career is beginning and your salary is small. Plan these twelve basic pieces around one of Spring's Authority Colors, like taupe or bright navy, plus a color from your palette, like sage or apricot. Then build up to the mid-level and top-level wardrobes appropriate to your profession. You can always add another color from your palette as your career and your wardrobe needs grow. But you'll be astounded at how many different outfits you can create from the first 1 + 1 Professional Wardrobe you purchase:

❏ One all-weather overcoat with a zip-out lining
❏ One blazer
❏ One cardigan sweater
❏ Two turtlenecks or mock turtleneck tops
❏ Two blouses, one with tie
❏ One pair of slacks
❏ One mid-length skirt
❏ One knee-length skirt
❏ One over-sized sweater
❏ One vest (use Chapter 5 to determine length according to height and weight)

Spring's 1 + 1 Wardrobe Combinations

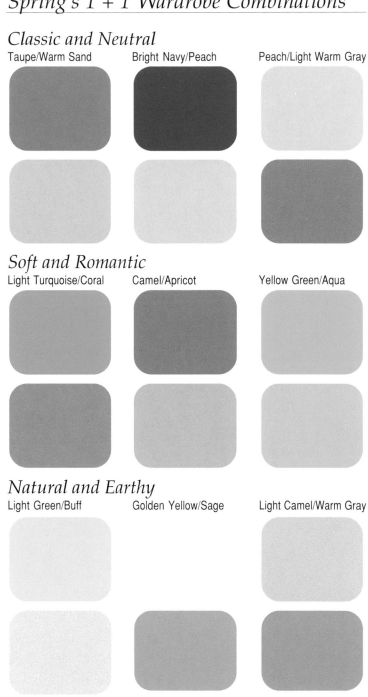

Classic and Neutral

Taupe/Warm Sand   Bright Navy/Peach   Peach/Light Warm Gray

Soft and Romantic

Light Turquoise/Coral   Camel/Apricot   Yellow Green/Aqua

Natural and Earthy

Light Green/Buff   Golden Yellow/Sage   Light Camel/Warm Gray

Color Personality

*N*ature has defined your best colors, and the seasonal color theory will help you identify them and show you new ones to try for business and pleasure. There's no doubt that a radiant appearance can influence the development of your personality. Look at the range of sparkling personalities revealed by Paula, Jenny, Collette, and Marcia. Winters Jenny and Collette are as vivid and dramatic as their coloring. Paula and Marcia, both Autumns, are as warm, earthy, and energetic as they look.

Collette

Dark, dramatic Winter Collette is as intense as her coloring. Winters command our attention with their vivid contrasts. They are as sparkling as ice; as fiery as an open fire; as dramatic as a stark winter landscape. Their vitality makes them exciting performers.

Altomease

Soft, gentle Summer Altomease is as dreamy and creative as she looks. Summer's soft features and translucent skin make her seem as comforting as a warm summer breeze and as calm as a deep, cool lake. Her flexible nature makes her a good friend and loyal companion.

Color Personality

Karen

Warm, earthy Karen is a rich, vital Autumn. Autumns are as energetic as leaves swirling in the wind, as warm as the first rays of September. Their strength often takes them into leadership roles.

Edda

Delicate, bright Spring Edda blooms with health and energy, like an athlete. Flirtatious, airy, and free, Springs need high energy careers, full of creativity and adventure. With their full palette of colors, they are artistic and flamboyant.

Text continues from page 76

Dress for Work, not Play

Wanda, referred to me by a client who had been one of my makeover successes, is a support assistant for a major corporation. She is a very beautiful African-American woman, but she dressed as if she were going to a cocktail party directly after work! Low-cut dresses, rhinestone hose, and strappy shoes with heels, toes, and sides cut out were her usual fare. She wore her hair up with ornaments throughout, and her makeup colors did not complement her skin tone.

To make matters worse, Wanda had been denied promotion three times. Why? Because throughout the work day, she fixed, fussed, and played with her makeup five out of the eight hours. She couldn't work for taking breaks to rearrange her hair ornaments. Wanda agreed that she needed a full color and wardrobe analysis. First, we discovered she was a Spring. Then I convinced her that the evening look she had favored on the job must be reserved for after work. When that was accomplished, we organized her closet together so that she had evening clothing in one section, casual clothing in another, and work clothing in still another.

Wanda and I went shopping for accessories, hosiery, shoes, makeup, belts, and jewelry. We stayed within her budget and accomplished a great deal. It was difficult for her, but once she understood that less time spent on fussing with her look meant more time spent on the company operations and her success within the company, she warmed up to the changes.

I do not see Wanda often, but she is climbing the success ladder and feeling good about herself and much more a part of her organization. Self-motivation is the key to becoming successful, and Wanda was willing to make a change. She looked around and wondered why and how others became successful, and she sought help.

People who work with Wanda speak to her differently now, and respect her work. She is no longer hassled by turned-on men and does not primp all day without getting down to business. She is no longer late to work. Now, she organizes her outfits at night, including accessories, and goes to bed feeling at ease about the day to come. What a relief!

Charting Your Five-Year Cycle

So, what's all the fuss about beauty and how it relates to success? Let's take a moment to organize our priorities. Ask yourself: Is how I dress my company's business? It shouldn't be, but it is. If you are good at what you do, your boss approves of your work. But your appearance needs to reflect that success. Every five years you should chart the course of your career and academic success and analyze whether your wardrobe has kept up with you. Answer the following questions honestly:

1. Is my appearance getting me through the door?

2. What are my clothes saying to others?

3. Do I feel comfortable in front of a group?

4. Am I shopping because I am bored and don't have a clue what style of clothing best suits me?

5. Do I have enough "working" pieces to mix and match in my current wardrobe?

Based on your answers to these questions, you should be able to determine if you need to enhance and improve on your appearance.

How My Wardrobe Changed with My Career

The great American dream is to be financially independent and to build something special for yourself. That has been my own goal for the last fifteen years. I have had to endure adversity along the way, but thanks to believing in a higher power and seeking direction, I've been able to overcome the obstacles. I've learned commitment and sacrificed to become a successful woman of color.

Let me show you how my own personal wardrobe changed as my career path did. I began my career with a very basic wardrobe built around a mid-length black flair skirt and an oversized sweater, worn with opaque stockings for daytime and sheer stockings for evening. Soon I added one red and one black blazer. Gradually, I added a navy blue suit, blazer, slacks, and skirt, and wore these with four additional blouses and one sweater.

Within another two years, I became active in organizations for business women. Then I added a chic black gabardine suit with silver buttons worn with a white silk blouse, and one gray gabardine shirt dress with silver buttons down the front and a black crepe collar. Next I invested in a gabardine overcoat and a stunning red suit that had just enough flair to separate it from the traditional business suit. All along I was married to black and navy pumps, varying the height of the heels and leather—suede for fall and patent leather for summer.

Be a Woman

The woman executive who thinks that she needs a closet full of tailored masculine suits, complete with a man's style shirt and tie, or a soft necktie for each ruffled blouse, is making a huge mistake. Women are attractive *and* appropriate at the office in dresses, soft feminine slacks, skirts, and blouses, sweater and skirt combinations, and suits cut with soft lines that contour your body shape and size. A woman working in a man's arena need not imitate men's fashions. Instead, be proud to look like a woman. Looking like a woman makes the men around you much more relaxed, and you are treated with the utmost respect. You will end up finding it easier to work with them.

The Small But Efficient Wardrobe

What is the ideal wardrobe? We all have our concept of the ideal wardrobe and it usually involves volume. We have dreamed of having all the clothes we want at our disposal whenever we so choose.

Your dream might be like this. Three of your favorite designers and their assistants come to your house once a month. They bring with them their newest fashion ideas for you to preview. Thousands of dresses, blouses, sweaters, blazers, slacks, and shoes in the most stunning colors—suited to your color palette, of course—and styles are displayed just for you.

You choose from this selection of beautiful clothing and your designers coordinate striking accessories for each outfit. Not only do you have all the clothes you could possibly wear, but the finished, custom look is guaranteed because the accessories are perfect.

Instead of having several things to wear, you own thousands—your own little boutique. Instead of choosing an outfit to suit the occasion, you simply indulge your every mood: a luxurious royal blue skirt and oversized top with matching belt for the theater, a jogging suit with matching sneakers to carpool the children to dance class, and a velour pants suit for a birthday party at home with family and friends.

What a dream! But in reality, neither I nor you have such a clothing advantage, and we don't need one to be happy and well dressed. My best advice to you is to forget the clothes fantasy and adopt the idea of a small, realistic, but efficient wardrobe.

We tend to want more clothing than will make us happy in the first place. Usually, we over-consume, then we are dissatisfied and frustrated. A much better approach is to know that there is a limit to the number of outfits you can use efficiently.

Decide what your style is and stick to it. You'll find you can build your wardrobe over the years by buying basic styles made of the best fabric and, of course, replacing or repairing them when they are worn. For example, my navy Ellen Tracy blazer is eight years old. I still use it as a base for adding pieces. Then adopt the principles in Chapter 7 and treat yourself to accessories. With this approach, you will always be well dressed, elegant and stunning. You'll be less frustrated and spend less time and money. Stop thinking lots of clothes and start thinking of the small, successful, and efficient wardrobe.

How 1 + 1 Can Equal the Professional Wardrobe for You

Here is the ultimate wardrobe, based on 1 + 1 color combinations, that I've developed over the years as I've counseled hundreds of career women.

Every woman needs authority on the job, and a carefully built professional wardrobe can help you achieve the look that says you mean what you say and you know what you're talking about. Start with one Authority Color from your palette. Authority Colors are darker. For Winters, black is best, but dark navy is also authoritative. Summers can use navy, but flannel gray is also outstanding. Autumns should take aubergine or dark brown for their Authority Color, while Springs should choose taupe or bright navy. Now select one other color from your palette—any color you enjoy wearing and you know makes you look and feel good.

This is your 1 + 1 color combination.

Take this 1 + 1 color combination and use it to build your Professional Wardrobe. Start with twelve basic pieces of clothing in these two colors, when your career is beginning and your salary is small, and you'll be astounded at how many different outfits you'll have, right from the beginning. Build up to the mid-level and top-level wardrobes, adding another color from your palette if you choose, as your career grows. If your job doesn't require you to wear skirts and tailored slacks, use the tips on accessories in Chapter 7 to best complement your uniforms or other required attire. Refer to your own Wardrobe List from Chapter 1 and fill in the blanks of the appropriate chart for your career level to see what you have and what you need. When you shop, take your chart and your palette with you so you'll never again make an expensive mistake.

With these twelve basic pieces in your 1 + 1 color combination, you've purchased the wardrobe you need to get you started. Combine them in different ways to create outfits, and use Chapter 7 to select the best accessories to vary the look of these pieces.

Basic Twelve Wardrobe for Beginning Your Professional Career

❑ **One all-weather overcoat with a zip-out lining**

❑ **One blazer**

❑ **One cardigan sweater**

❑ **Two turtlenecks or mock turtleneck tops**

❑ **Two blouses, one with a tie**

❑ **One pair of slacks**

❑ **One mid-length skirt**

❑ **One knee-length skirt**

❑ **One oversized sweater**

❑ **One vest (use Chapter 5 to determine length)**

Mid-Level Manager

As you move up the career ladder and your professional activities and salary increase, you can augment your 1 + 1 Professional Wardrobe with the following items. Don't forget accessories (see Chapter 7).

- ❑ **One wool coat**
- ❑ **Two daytime suits**
- ❑ **One sweater blazer**
- ❑ **Three blouses**
- ❑ **One basic dressy dress**
- ❑ **One pair of slacks**

Top-Level Manager

The top-level manager should not feel she can toss all caution (and therefore money) to the wind. She must be just as smart and organized in shopping for her wardrobe. Remember to vary fabric weights and use accessories to accent your outfits. Add the following items:

- ❑ **One dressy all-weather coat with a zip-out lining**
- ❑ **Two signature blazers or jackets**
- ❑ **Two skirts**
- ❑ **Three blouses**
- ❑ **Two basic daytime dresses**
- ❑ **One short cocktail dress**
- ❑ **One ankle- or floor-length evening dress**

My Professional Wardrobe

Complete the chart on the next page to determine what you have and what you need to buy.

Build your wardrobe around some of the 1 + 1 color combinations suggested for your season on pages 77 to 85 and your own palette for a third color.

Entry-Level Basic Twelve
in 1 + 1 Color Combination

1 + 1 Color Combination _____

	WHAT I HAVE	WHAT I NEED	COLOR
One all-weather overcoat	☐	☐	_____
One blazer	☐	☐	_____
One cardigan	☐	☐	_____
Two turtlenecks or mock turtleneck tops	☐	☐	_____
Two blouses, one with a tie	☐	☐	_____
One pair of slacks	☐	☐	_____
One mid-length skirt	☐	☐	_____
One knee-length skirt	☐	☐	_____
One oversized sweater	☐	☐	_____
One vest	☐	☐	_____

Mid-Level Manager

1 + 1 + 1 Color Combination_____

	WHAT I HAVE	WHAT I NEED	COLOR
One wool coat	☐	☐	_____
Two daytime suits	☐	☐	_____
One sweater blazer	☐	☐	_____
Three blouses	☐	☐	_____
One basic dressy dress	☐	☐	_____
One pair of slacks	☐	☐	_____

Top-Level Manager

1 + 1 + 1 Color Combination _____

	What I Have	What I Need	Color
One fur coat	☐	☐	_____
One signature blazer or jacket	☐	☐	_____
One skirt	☐	☐	_____
Three blouses	☐	☐	_____
Two basic dresses	☐	☐	_____
One short cocktail dress	☐	☐	_____
One ankle- or floor-length evening dress	☐	☐	_____

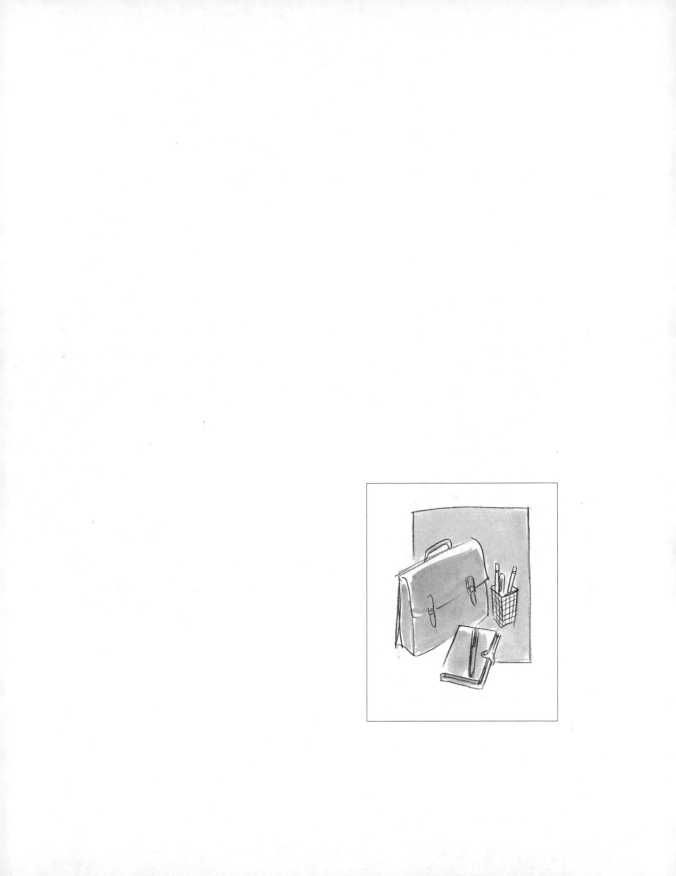

CHAPTER 4
A New Hair Color, a New You

Sara, a lovely Chinese American, attended a workshop I was conducting for professional women. She is a forty-two-year-old banker who needed a conservative business look.

She approached me after the meeting and told me that she was totally unhappy with the appearance and condition of her hair. It hung long and limp down her back, was damaged, and had no real style because she had been cutting it herself. She also requested my assistance with her makeup, wardrobe colors, and accessories.

I began her makeover with a color analysis. She is a striking Winter who had been wearing grays and beiges and wondering why her appearance was lackluster. When we found clear red, lemon yellow, black frost, and emerald green blouses and accessories, she began to look as dynamic as she felt inside.

Next, I cut her hair. Wow! Did that make a difference! Sara told me that it was the first time she had ever had a cut that she liked. We emphasized the shiny straightness and thickness of her hair, as well as the lovely oval of her face, by giving her a blunt cut, which gently curved under her chin and brushed her shoulders. She looked younger and more sophisticated, self-assured, and in control of her destiny.

Then I changed her entire line of cosmetics. Because Sara had oily, blemished skin, I established a full cleansing routine and recommended a corrective plan for her. After several months, her skin showed definite improvement. She is now a regular client for both hair care and cosmetics, and she has faithfully kept her appointments for the last two years.

I am now assisting her with the selection of basic wardrobe pieces and accessories. We have similar tastes in clothes, and she respects and appreciates my efforts to do advance shopping for her.

Two Deadly Sins

Sara has only two remaining faults—both of which stem from her general lack of patience and her occasional impulse to change her appearance and grooming habits. First, she needs to begin a regimen for improving the condition of her nails. She says that she has had sculptured nails in the past, but she doesn't have the patience to have them done regularly. She frequently removed them after a couple of days because "they just got on my nerves." I hope that I will ultimately be able to convince her to get regular manicures and change the way she uses her hands so that she can have beautiful natural nails.

Second, she occasionally pops into a mall for a haircut by someone she doesn't know. On two occasions, I had to recut a bad cut she received in between her scheduled appointments. The last cut she received was really radical; she had her hair cut short and she lost most of the hair at her nape and sides. She has regretted this so extensively that she *may* be cured!

Luckily, her hair is growing back again in luxuriant health.

Your Signature for Success

Your hair is your signature and completes your total look. Imagine walking into a room full of prospective clients dressed in your best Calvin Klein suit, but with your hair neglected and dull. It detracts from you. Oh, how you wish you'd kept your appointment with your stylist! You spent too much on your outfit, so maybe there wasn't enough money for your crowning glory, your signature for success. *Never* again.

If you are in search of your dream job and you are not a hair person, spend a little time researching your image and how it could fit into that company structure. In this chapter I'll show you how your season will make coloring and managing your hair easy.

Three Hairstyle Rules

When you choose a hairstyle, there are three things you must take into consideration: *personal look*, *lifestyle*, and *texture of hair*. If you are thinking of changing your hair color, consider the pros and cons before you do anything. There are many hair colors you can buy in the drugstore, but do you really know which colors give you clarity, evenness, and a natural glow? Which are the colors that make your skin, eyes, and total appearance reflect your seasonal palette and personality the best?

Your hair is as much a part of your style as your clothes.

Artists like Diana Ross, Patti LaBelle, Shari Belafonte, Sade, and Iman have changed their hairstyles to complement their fashion statements. They have professionals to help them do it.

Maybe you, in your busy nine-to-five world, have not taken the time to consult a professional and dashed into the use of unknown hair products to alter the natural texture or color of your hair. In a frustrated frenzy, you may even have chopped your hair off rather than wait for an appointment. If so, you've learned the hard way that there is more to creating a new hairstyle than bankers, teachers, students, or architects know!

Color Your Hair Beautiful

Color is one of the most dramatic and effective ways to enhance your hair and your total look, giving your skin tone a harmonious appearance. When consulting a stylist about hair coloring, ask about these three basic color products.

Temporary Colors. Temporary colors come in mousses, gels, and rinses. These coat the hair rather than penetrate the new growth shafts, and usually wash out with the very next shampoo. Because temporary color does not cover evenly and does not lighten, color shampoos are good between permanent coloring.

Semi-permanent Colors. These also coat the hair with color, but they cover better and last at least through four to six shampoos. These deposit coloring to the shaft of the hair, lifting rather than depositing color. But be careful if you shampoo often; your hair color may not look the same from one day to the next.

Permanent Colors. Permanent hair color works by penetrating the new growth shaft to lift rather than deposit new hair color. Permanent hair coloring is used to change natural color, or to lighten, darken, or cover gray. Color touch-ups depend on how fast the hair grows. Too much coloring, and coloring used incorrectly, can damage your hair.

I prefer semi-permanent hair coloring to vegetable rinses that usually fade after a few shampoos and generally distort the natural color. Semi-permanent hair coloring deposits color into the hair, while permanent hair coloring lifts and then deposits color into the hair. This semi-color process is not as harsh and the results are rich in coloring while the hair remains healthy. Also, this process cuts peroxide use in half.

Find the Right Stylist

It is worth the time and trouble it takes to find the right hair stylist. It can make such a difference in the way you look. I recommend finding an unpretentious local salon that is willing to work with you and your hair. Investigate salons that have celebrity clients. Often these salons can and will cater to you and will give healthy hair the attention it deserves. Usually, the staff is informed and trained to provide each service listed on the menu. Just look at the celebrity list; it should reflect the image provided to each client.

Once you find a stylist you like, make your first appointment a *consultation* session only. Be sure to state clearly what you have in mind. You need professional help before altering your color or style, and the key to satisfaction is effective communication between the client and stylist.

The perfect style cannot be cut and pasted to your face. Your facial features play a very important role in accomplishing the right look. The perfect color does not come from one bottle of coloring. It takes talent and experience to create the right look for you. A trained cosmetologist will blend several colors to create the color that is perfect for you.

The Perfect Color for You

Choosing the right color should not be left to trial and error. It may (and may not) be true that blondes have more fun and redheads are hot, but these hair colors can ruin your personal look if they aren't in your seasonal palette. A trained cosmetologist will look at your skin and not only see brown, beige, or pink, but also will see your tones of blue, green, yellow, and red. These tones, combined with your natural eye color, will help you choose the right shade of black, brown, red, gray, or blond.

For those of you who don't want to make a permanent commitment to any one color, there are vegetable and cellophane rinses. Many women start with a rinse to see if they like a color. Rinses lie on top of the hair shaft and rinse out a little with every shampoo.

Once you and your stylist decide on the right color, it is time to move to a permanent color and style. A permanent color will not wash out, but you *will* need to be touched up at the roots of your hair as your hair grows.

Winters. Most often, Winters have dark brown to black hair. A Winter person should *never* frost, streak, or bleach her hair. Artificial frosting is a definite no-no; it takes away from nature's placement of each strand of your hair. It is rare to find a Winter who looks good with her hair bleached, frosted, or highlighted. A Winter also should never use red/

orange or red/yellow combinations in her hair, so please don't let anyone tell you differently!

I recommend Winters use semi-permanent or permanent hair coloring—darkest brown or black for dark color hair, and pearl, steel, or platinum for gray hair. Often I add a mahogany cast or tint to Winters who have chemically treated their hair with perms and relaxers. With both the correct makeup and right silver accessories, the look works.

For Winters who are in doubt as to what to do with their long or short salt-and-pepper hair, choose a hair length and style that suit your life-style and overall personality. Salt-and-pepper Winters really shouldn't color their hair; it has so much body and vivacity. Instead of spending money on incorrect coloring, spend it on the right hair-care advice to enhance your total look. By all means, avoid those labels with the word "warm."

Note: If your hair is a little red or if red tones appear from chemical treatments, have your stylist give you a toner or a rinse with a cool base.

Summers. Frosting is a great way for Summers to add zest to their total look. If Summers choose frosting, they should always use a blue or purple base to avoid a green, orange, or red cast to the hair. Summers gray very beautifully and should leave the gray natural or use blended highlights throughout the hair. They should also avoid labels that read "warm." Because of the intense red pigments in their skin, only a few Summers can have a reddish cast to their hair. The red clashes with their skin and makes them look tired or harsh.

Suggested Hair Coloring

Winter

Violet base   Darkest brown
Blue base   Black
Ash brown

Summer

Light ash brown   Frosting
Ash brown   Dark brown

Autumn

Golden blond   Red
Blond brown   Reddish brown
Dark gold   Strawberry
Chestnut brown

Note: If you are graying slowly, cover completely.

Spring

Light golden brown   Winter wheat
Medium golden brown   Reddish brown
Golden brown   Strawberry blond
Flaxen blond

Note: If you are graying slowly, cover completely.

Autumns. Healthy, rich, luscious, brown, red, or auburn hair comes alive with proper care. The Autumn woman looks great in her natural red and gold highlights.

I provide a lot of custom blending of hair coloring to enhance the skin tone of women of color. Most women cannot achieve a personal look from one bottle of color. Often Autumns need to enhance their deep-brown hair because chemical processing such as perms and relaxers have left a red film on the hair, creating the wrong contrasts for Autumn. I recommend a toner to remove the red and return the hair to its richer, golden color.

But unlike her cool Winter and Summer sisters, the Autumn woman who wants to age gracefully *should* cover the gray in her hair. In doing so, remember that most Autumn women have red to warm-toned hair coloring and should avoid ash tones.

Springs. Many Spring women have warm blonde to brown hair that may be darkened to a golden shade that looks naturally beautiful. Most often, Springs need a little lift to keep the spark alive in their hair. Why? Because chemical treatment, body waves, perms, and cigarette smoke in the air tend to leave a cast on the hair, making it dull and lifeless. So I recommend using a flaxen, winter wheat, or golden hair rinse to enhance Spring's natural hair coloring.

Springs should be very careful when frosting their hair. Too much ash can make them look a lot older than they really are. The Spring woman's hair does not gray attractively. I recommend they seek professional advice on coloring. Springs can use many shades of the golden and auburn family, but a professional hair stylist can best determine which color is best.

Health for Your Hair

Once you have your new look, the real work begins. For all the beauty color adds to the hair, it also takes away a lot of moisture. Be certain to have your stylist use a deep conditioner on your hair after each shampoo. Between shampoos, a light moisturizing lotion should be added to help keep the luster in your hair.

Hair loss is never an easy thing to handle. It can be emotionally upsetting for any woman. Society puts such an awful amount of pressure on us to look good. One form of hair loss is Alopecia, which usually occurs during the early twenties from a combination of three factors: heredity, age, and testosterone. Another cause is excessive use of the curling iron, which can damage your hair so extensively that hair loss occurs.

But don't worry. Your beautician can help with reconstructive treatments, scalp treatments, and even hair weaving or replacement. *Spend the money and get professional help.* You'll feel and look much better.

The women who frequent my salon are not aspiring singers or actors and are not looking for purple or green hair. We specialize in giving the professional woman an added advantage in the boardroom. So if you are a supernova in your own universe, it's important to create new hairstyles and hair coloring for *you*, using your color palette. Let hair color add to your style.

Orlene is an African-American Summer who was referred to me by her sister. Orlene had been to several salons, trying to find one that would take interest in her desire to develop a more polished and professional image. Grooming and a holistic approach to beauty were important to her.

I immediately determined Orlene was in need of a step-by-step makeover in order to accomplish the total look she wanted. I started with a shaping haircut and regular intensive hair conditioning. Gradually, I added facials, a new line of facial cleaners, highlights for her brunette hair, and manicures and pedicures into her beauty regime.

Orlene's hair became healthier and a graduated cut gave her more volume. Her skin is glowing and she is now a woman in tune with beauty routines that give her a sophisticated yet fresh appearance.

Now That You've Colored It, Cut It

As we've discussed, once you've found your hair's color palette, take the next step with your stylist and find the perfect cut for your life-style and face shape. A good haircut should be easy to maintain between appointments and continue to look good.

If you have a round face, wear your hair shoulder length, but layer the top and sides, making sure the layered hair blends with the longer hair. Blunt cuts and a long-layered, softly pulled-back style are great for you. But if you top your hair with a fringe, chances are your face will appear rounder. Better to angle your hair back on both sides, or curve it to the side over one eye.

If you have a round face to begin with, be careful about any weight gain. I remember when I was feeling bored with my looks and had gained twenty unwanted pounds. I thought cutting my hair would make me look thinner. Instead, I ended up looking much heavier than I really was because the cut emphasized the shape of my face, which had really become round. So, ladies, don't think of cutting your hair to distract from any weight gain. Cut your weight by starting that exercise and diet program you've been avoiding!

If you have a heart-shaped face, you can wear shoulder-length hairstyles, too. You should have your hair cut bluntly and wear it curly or blown-dry straight or full. If you wear your hair short, it will emphasize your heart-shaped face by drawing attention to your pointed chin and away from your pretty eyes.

If you have a square face, add some bangs to play down the size of your forehead. Have your stylist custom blend your long or short style concentrating on your eyes, cheekbones, and jawbone to structure a cut and style.

If your face is long, don't try to wear long dramatic styles. They will only emphasize the length of your face and make it look angular. Try a layered shoulder-length style with a half bang to give you a softer, more youthful look. Or try a short sassy cut. I've had clients tell me I've taken ten years off their appearance just by cutting their hair and giving them an opportunity to wear those big, bold earrings.

If you have a low forehead, wear your hair brushed back from your face. And keep any bangs light and wispy. Wear a full hairstyle if you have a large nose, and never wear it pulled severely back. To disguise a double chin, wear your hair in a bob or pageboy.

Pay attention as your stylist creates your hairdo. It will help you when you style it yourself. But more importantly, watch what's happening to your hair simply because it will put you in control. I can't tell you how many times I've had new clients complain about how their previous stylist sat them with their back to the mirror. Once the cutting was completed and they were whirled around to see the results, they were disappointed.

We are all individuals with our own unique gifts, looks, and facial features. That's why it is so very important to establish a relationship with one or two stylists in a salon, so that you will not get a haircut designed for someone else.

Know Your Hair's Texture

Your stylist will consider the texture of your hair and its natural curls, waves, or straightness when he or she designs your hairdo. Don't fight the natural tendencies of your hair; enhance them, so your heritage works for you, not against you.

Fine, curly hair looks better in a full natural style, while coarse hair works best with a straight style. If your hair texture is coarse and uncontrollable, you may want to use a hair straightener to keep it relaxed so that it won't overcome your face. Remember Chelsea Clinton before her father took office? Or President Clinton, for that matter. Both had very coarse, thick hair that was out of control. What about Lani Guinier, the controversial University of Pennsylvania professor who was criticized not only for her civil rights opinions but also for her "big hair"? All three have obviously found excellent beauty consultants who provided them with more appropriate hair styles.

Hair straighteners come in liquid form and chemically rearrange the natural structure of curly hair. Relaxers do the same thing as straighteners, but the look is much more gentle, resulting in soft curls or waves.

A permanent curls your hair by breaking down the chemical bonds that shape your hair, altering the form to make a wave pattern set by different-sized rods or curlers on your head. But don't try to give yourself a permanent, or ask a friend to do it for you. You'll be sorry and so will your hair—that is, if you don't lose it all! So please, see your stylist.

Cut to Your Lifestyle

Elena, an energetic Latin-American Winter, is one of our happiest clients. She started with our skin care specialist, then decided she needed the works. Her law practice keeps her frantic, and she needs to be ready for every occasion, from meeting the president of a corporation to pleading a landmark case. I began her hair-care treatment by giving her a temporary rinse to enhance her skin tone, then styled her hair in a short tapered cut that exactly fits her busy schedule and her oval face, and is sophisticated enough to give her a polished professional look.

Elena tells me often that this cut gave her the confidence she needs to make formal presentations and that with it she can count on always looking her best. We've had to make some adjustments to fit her in at a moment's notice, but that's what a good stylist does—and don't you forget it.

CHAPTER 5
Trouble Spots

I have advised many women of color over many years, and every single one of them has the same complaint: at least one figure flaw that prevents them from being beautiful. Some feel they are too tall, others are too short. Most feel they are too fat, a few are too thin. Others complain that their bust is too big...or too little. We all have a list of what we think are our figure problems. I have never met a woman who doesn't.

But stop and look around you. There are many people who are attractive but who are less than perfect. They've learned to accommodate their figure flaws through skillful use of color and wardrobe building. Now you can, too.

The style of clothing you select—its color, line, shape, texture, and pattern—can do much to camouflage your flaws or even change your total appearance. You can't actually change your shape, but you *can* hide your flaws and accentuate your assets.

As we know, color is the most important element in selecting your clothing and enhancing your natural beauty. Almost on its own, it can disguise and distract from figure flaws. But there are also some "tricks" of line, shape, texture, and pattern that can create the illusion of the figure you want. Remember, always wear clothes that fit; they should neither be too tight nor too loose. Choose carefully, get professional help if need be, and be proud of what you've got. You'll look great and get the compliments you deserve.

Here are some hints to help.

Height

Too Tall. Tall women should wear bright, bold colors from their palette with vivid contrasting accessories. They can wear horizontal stripes and patterns, too.

Scarves can be a terrific accessory for breaking height; they focus the eye on the vivid colors around your neck. Full sleeves and draped or cowled necklines can also camouflage areas where you are too thin, and they help relieve the long lines of height. Choose bulky or textured fabrics and full skirts with gathered waistlines. Wide pants, full skirts, and tall boots can help disguise legs that are thin or too large.

If you are tall and full-figured, avoid anything that adds *too* much height: vertical stripes, solid-colored outfits in dark muted shades, and clinging fabrics. Ruffles can sometimes soften figure lines that are too long, but they are *definitely not* for full-figured women.

Height

Too Short. Short women are often unaware of their advantages. They are usually well-proportioned and can wear almost anything their tall sisters can. Nowadays, the same fashions are available in the petite section of the store. Muted colors are good choices because they make you appear taller than you really are. But you'll do well in bright colors, too, if you are petite.

To add height, wear clothes that are all the same color or different shades of the same color. You also should wear your belts a little lower than your waistline. Hosiery and shoes of the same color as your skirt will give the illusion of a tall, thin silhouette.

Hem length is crucial to shorter women. If you *must* wear long skirts, make sure they are not too long. If you wear your skirts a little shorter than current fashion dictates, it's to your advantage. Adding a jacket to your outfit can also make you seem leaner, especially if it is the same color as your skirt or pants.

Weight

Too Heavy. Do you have a large bone structure or are you overweight? I have a friend who wears stunning clothing with tasteful shoes to match. She wears a size eighteen and looks fantastic. Her positive attitude and sense of style enhance her appearance.

If you are heavier than the average, put together outfits in different tones of the same color, rather than of contrasting ones. Choose lines that are smooth and uncluttered. Don't be tempted to wear tight clothing: it will make you appear larger.

Nowadays, buying clothing can be fun for the full-figured woman because designers and manufacturers have finally admitted that many of us *are* bigger than a size fourteen. It's about time they learned to accommodate the various sizes and body shapes of the world's women. So, if you are a little larger than you'd like, "shed" some pounds by wearing the colors in your seasonal palette and those tailored styles and subtle, vertical patterns that can help you look thinner faster than a crash diet.

Weight

Too Thin. Bright colors from your palette, horizontal stripes, vivid patterns, and textured fabrics will make you look more substantial. But avoid your dark colors, especially worn together. You can wear the most extravagant accessories—scarves, jewelry, belts, and shoes—if that is your style—for they will add to your frame. If not, be a little more self-confident, and start wearing well-chosen scarves and belts. See Chapter 7 for some further suggestions.

Bustlines

Too Big. If your bust is larger than you would like, wear fun accessories near your face and away from your bust. Soft draped or cowled collars will also lead the eye where you want it. Be sure to choose colors from your palette and avoid those horizontal lines or too much draping around your chest. Also, no double-breasted dresses or jackets. The double-breasted cut will make you appear wider. And never wear lighter colored blouses with dark slacks or skirts, for this tends to emphasize your bustline.

Bustlines

Too Small. If your bust is smaller than you'd like, wear lots of detailing, patterns, ruffles, or horizontal stripes on your tops. You can also wear full sleeves and A-line dresses to disguise and soften your bustline.

Hips

Too Large. If your hips are larger than you would like, again, use color to draw attention away from this part of your body. Wear your most vivid colors on top, and muted colors below. Avoid buying pants and skirts with pockets and pleats. Wear a loose-fitting jacket, vest, or tunic to simulate a straight line. You'll look a lot slimmer in loose-fitting clothing, gracefully covered by a jacket, vest, or coat. The longer vests are very fashionable and can look stunning. If your waist is tiny, please do not wear a tight wide belt: it will emphasize your hips!

Hips

Too narrow. Jackets and vests also disguise too narrow hips by adding balance to your outfit. Wear your bright colors below, and muted or neutral colors above. You can wear big belts, wide-legged pants, and/ or exciting boots to draw the eye away from your hips.

Waist

Too Big. If your waist is too large, hide it with straight-lined looks. Wear blazers and vests to add length. Try belts in the same color as your outfit—never in a contrasting color that emphasizes your waist. Wear vivid accessories near your face, and the same-colored tops and bottoms.

Short-waisted. Women who are short-waisted should also wear clothing that creates the illusion of height. For example, wear long vests, sweaters, and oversized shirts over your pants and skirts. Please don't wear wide waistbands; they make your waistline appear even shorter.

Waist

Long-waisted. Tall, thin women often are also long-waisted. Wear full, soft tops rather than tight, fitted blouses. You look glamorous in wide belts and cummerbunds, with your blouse or top tugged snugly inside.

Too Small. Can a waist ever be too small? Show it off with wide bright colored belts and cummerbunds in heavy fabrics.

A Good Fit

You'll find that clothes that fit you—in style and size—are your best bet for looking your very best. Don't be embarrassed to ask a professional shopper for help at your favorite clothing store.

A good fit is 90 percent of the image game when it comes to clothing. Even the most expensive clothing will not complement your total look if the fit is incorrect. So do not make the mistake of buying clothing that is too large or too small. Learn to take a critical look in the mirror; identify your assets and your defects, and *maximize* your strong points.

Remember, color is *free*. Using it well and wisely will cost you no more than using it poorly. The key is to recognize that color has a tremendous impact on you, your self-esteem, and the people around you.

The Figure Troubleshooter Chart

Problem	Solutions				
	Colors	Texture	Stripes	Patterns	Shape
Height					
Too tall	**Bright**	**Heavy**	**Horizontal**	**Vivid**	**Full**
Too short	**Muted**	**Smooth**	**Vertical**	**Soft**	**Fitted**
Weight					
Too heavy	**Muted**	**Smooth**	**Vertical**	**Soft**	**Loose**
Too thin	**Bright**	**Heavy**	**Horizontal**	**Vivid**	**Full**
Bust					
Too full	**Muted**	**Smooth**	**Vertical**	**Soft**	**Loose**
Too small	**Vivid**	**Heavy**	**Horizontal**	**Vivid**	**Full ruffles**
Hips					
Too wide	**Muted**	**Smooth**	**Vertical**	**Soft**	**Straight**
Too small	**Bright**	**Heavy**	**Horizontal**	**Vivid**	**Loose**
Waist					
Too wide	**Muted**	**Smooth**	**Vertical**	**None**	**Thin**
Too small	**Bright**	**Heavy**	**Horizontal**	**Vivid**	**Wide**

CHAPTER 6

Smart Shopping

The rapid entry of women into the work world over the last twenty years, and especially the increase of professional women, has changed not only women's shopping priorities but also their shopping strategies and habits.

Each Business Has Its Own Dress Code

There is an art to dressing well for the workplace. Now that you're an artist, you can "paint" a wardrobe to frame your career. In a sense, each business has its own dress code. There is no doubt that an executive's success in business can be hindered if she doesn't dress the part. It may seem unfair that the veneer is so important, but it is a fact of life. A person dressed appropriately and in quality clothing projects a strong image for her profession. If the fashion is good, everyone notices.

Each time you dress for an occasion—especially a business occasion—you must go through the decision-making process. You must select, accessorize, and organize yourself so that you will arrive properly dressed and feeling confident. Your image is the key to your total personal presentation.

Before You Buy

Before buying a garment, always refer to your own 1 + 1 Professional Wardrobe checklist from Chapter 3, and ask yourself the following questions.

1. Considering my job and where I work, is this appropriate?

2. Is it in the right colors for my skin tone?

3. Is it good basic fashion or a fad?

4. Is it flattering to my body type?

5. Does it fit properly?

6. Is it right for this season?

7. Is it made of quality fabric and cut well enough to stay in my wardrobe for several seasons?

If you answer no to any of these questions, *don't buy it*. Always refer back to your checklist in Chapter 3 before purchasing anything, as well. If you really don't need the item, don't buy it. Buy another essential from your list instead.

The "Sale" Monster

Often, busy women see "Sale" and read it as "Buy." They believe they should buy the item no matter what color it is or what it may or may not match in their existing wardrobe or life-style. The sale is a monster for a woman who has little or no direction as to where she wants to be five years from now. I was once a sale victim. I would buy then and rationalize later. I forgot to ask: Is this color good for me? Do

I really need another black skirt? When you get swallowed up by the Sale Monster, you often discover you don't need all you bought. I've gotten home to discover the items I purchased didn't blend or coordinate with anything in my closet. Well, ladies, it is a struggle, but you *can* overcome the Sale Monster.

Your basic wardrobe will depend upon your career level, but you always should buy quality instead of quantity. And remember to choose your accessories while you are shopping for major items. In order to become more successful, you must not have to worry about buying an outfit for each occasion. You need to build and develop your dressing strategy *before* the actual occasion. You should be well-organized, and your basic style should be developed before you are up for that promotion or are about to launch your new business.

Panic Shopping

Have you ever shopped for an outfit the day before an event? We all fall prey to that anxiety. Suppose you receive a telephone call today from an important prospect. You are wanted in New York or California tomorrow to close the deal. Would you be ready?

I was. I received a call from my publicist on a Friday. She asked me to be in New York on Monday. I panicked. The first thing I thought was, "What do I take?" Then, "What should I wear?" Only then did I think about my presentation. And yet, my priority *must* be my presentation because I had identified, early in my career, what my fashion statement would be, and developed and expanded it and my wardrobe over the years. I was determined to be ready for the opportunity presented to me.

Let's Go Shopping

I must confess: I don't like shopping for long periods of time. I love having the right things to wear for any occasion, and I must have clothing that blends with my professional, personal, and social life. Therefore, I have become very systematic about shopping.

If your wardrobe needs extensive building, buy your major pieces first: *coats, suits, blazers, shoes, skirts, and shirts*.

Good Shopping Rules

Before learning my color season, I used to buy clothes impulsively. Something bright and colorful in a store would catch my eye. Many times, those purchases were mistakes; they hung in my closet, never worn, and reminded me that I was not an Autumn woman of color. Here is valuable shopping advice to help make your shopping trips productive.

1. **Only shop when you have time and energy.** Avoid shopping when you are tired and hungry. Organize yourself so that you don't lose time and money going from one shopping mall to the next.

2. **Remember that timing is everything.** It is best to shop early in the morning, on weekdays after the kids are off to school, after rush hour, and after a new season arrives. Get to know your sales representative. When items go on sale, she may notify you in advance and hold items until you are able to shop. Remember: sizes eight, ten, and twelve are hard to find.

3. **Wear comfortable, manageable clothes when you shop.** Wear clothes you can get into and out of easily. Avoid over-the-head

items that will ruin your makeup, hair, and articles you are think-ing about purchasing.

4. **Take it with you.** This is important if you are trying to match something, especially if the color is blue, black, red or orange-red. Whatever you do, *don't forget your portable color palette.*

5. **Buy clothes that are a good fit for you.** A good fit helps you look at ease and well put together. Know your trouble spots and which lines best camouflage them.

6. **Before you go shopping, know *what* you want to buy.** Make a list to save time.

I have a client, Margo, who shopped at three different Bloomingdale's, in three different shopping malls, in one day, to buy an item that could have been purchased within ten miles of her home. Her theory for going from shopping mall to shopping mall was that Store A, which is fifty miles away from her home, would have a skirt that matched the blazer she bought from Store B. At Store A, she dis-covered that Store C, which was closest to her home, had the only blouse that matched her suit.

What would you have done? How could you avoid running all over to shop?

The most reasonable and economical thing to do is to have your salesperson call Stores A and B and have the items sent to Store C.

Suppose you needed the items that same day?

In this case, you'll have to pick them up yourself, but at least the stores can put them on hold for you, so you or your best friend can pick them up quickly.

Fabrics

Like every woman, every fabric has its season—not the color season, but the time of year when it looks and feels best. Here are some of the major fabrics you'll find as the seasons progress.

Boucle
A slightly nubby wool or wool blend knit fabric, it is intended for autumn.

Broadcloth
A tightly woven smooth fabric, usually a cotton blend, it is just right for spring.

Challis
A soft, light- to medium-weight fabric with diagonal twill-like weave, it is made of wool, cotton, rayon, or a blend, and is perfect for winter.

Chiffon
A sheer, lightweight, flowing fabric, usually a silk blend, it drapes well in winter.

Cotton
A soft fabric made of tightly woven cotton fibers, it is worn in all seasons as a blouse, and as slacks, dresses, and jackets in summer.

Crepe
A lightweight fabric of silk, wool, or blend, it has a slightly raised or finely puckered surface and a matte finish. It is good for summer.

Crepe de Chine
Soft, lightweight silk or silk-blend crepe, it has a slightly raised surface and a matte finish. It is worn in all seasons and is perfect with accessories.

Denim
A coarse, twilled cloth, it is used for casual wear in all seasons.

Flannel   A cotton or wool fabric, it is medium to heavy with a slightly fuzzy, matte surface, it is for autumn and winter or on cool spring evenings.

Gabardine   A tightly woven diagonal twill, it comes in all weights. Usually a wool or wool blend, and even cotton, it is a good fabric for all four seasons and for travel.

Jersey   A soft, fine knit of cotton, wool, or blend, it has a matte finish and falls softly for spring or summer.

Linen   A fabric with a defined weave because of the sturdy threads, it comes in all weights and is best for summer. Linen is not a good travel fabric as it wrinkles easily.

Rayon   A synthetic texture similar to silk and satin, it can be worn in all seasons.

Satin   A smooth fabric blend of rayon and silk with a glossy front and dull back, it is a heavy fabric that works well for winter.

Silk   A lustrous fabric ranging from light and sheer to heavier chantung, it can be worn in all seasons.

Wool   A thick, soft, often curly-haired fabric, it varies in weight and texture depending on how it is woven, and is at its most comfortable when it is worn in autumn and winter.

Manage Your Closet—Don't Let It Manage You

I use my 1 + 1 Professional Wardrobe Chart as a closet manager checklist. I hang it on my closet door to help me keep inventory of what and how many individual items I have. I've noted the purchase date of important items, so I know when the old black turtleneck needs to be repaired or thrown out for a new one. I list the colors of hosiery in pencil to keep me from running out—which always seems to happen when I have a very busy schedule or am about to travel!

At the very least, use your own wardrobe chart to take a monthly inventory of what's inside. This way you will stay ahead of yourself and always be ready for any occasion.

Before you go shopping, remember to take a look at your inventory chart so that you replace any items that you've gotten rid of or sold to a consignment shop. This closet manager has prevented me—and my clients—from duplicating .

I had a client who bought the same style and color shirt *three times*, all in the same size. Each time Shayla went shopping, she was drawn to the same styles and colors—until we developed a closet manager for her.

A very dear client asked me for a color analysis and wardrobe consultation for her husband. With a lot of resistance, he allowed me in. I discovered he is a Winter, but greater than that, I realized men shop and manage their clothes worse than women. Tom had *eight* ties that are very similar in style and coloring. After I brought this to his attention, his response was, "Each time I am in a different city and visit the hotel stores, I buy the nicest tie I see. I change the tie I had on and wear the new one. I never realized I've purchased the same tie eight times in eight different cities!"

I had to share this male observation with you to show you how we are *all* programmed to one style and color. You feel that once you know your colors, you must stay within the spectrum. But that's why we image and color experts are here for you: to guide you from year to year, expanding your possibilities and helping you prevent life from growing dull, uneventful, or just plain boring.

Shopping for Your Career Cycle

I've had clients who return twice a year to coordinate and accessorize as they reach different plateaus in their lives. Several of my clients were resistant to the entire concept of color and dressing for success, but they have since accepted the facts: When you look good, you feel good, and you are more productive. So, ladies, take out your color palette and your wardrobe chart and get back on track if you've been on a buying spree. Stick to your chart—it's an *infallible* shopping list and closet manager.

High Style for Each Season

In my fifteen years of helping clients build wardrobes, I've found several designers who cater to specific seasons. For example, DKNY/ Donna Karan's navy blues, blacks, and grays are perfect for Winter and Summer women. The designer's whites usually work well for Spring or Autumn women.

Ellen Tracy's navy blues, whites, blacks, reds, and purples are just right for Winters and Summers. (However, her navy is a little too rich for Springs.) And for those women of the cool seasons who need a crisp white blouse, or one with black accents, Ellen Tracy is it: her whites are cool, not warm. She also makes a navy blazer with silver buttons that is a great wardrobe-builder for Winters and Summers.

For Autumn women, Dana Buchman makes a navy blazer with a hint of warmth and gold buttons. Dana Buchman's rich greens, golds, warm navy, and deep browns are definites for Autumns. And because of the warmth of this designer's hues, her clothing is also a must for Springs. I remember one occassion when I could not go shopping for my Autumn client, Jelka, a doctor from Calcutta. I sent her to Bloomingdale's with instructions not to try on anything but Dana Buchman. I saw her a few days later, just to make sure she had not invested $1,100 in pieces that were not perfect for her ultimate wardrobe. Well, everything fit her just right, was in her seasonal palette, and was an investment well spent.

Because of their perfect color choices, Ellen Tracy and Donna Karan are my two favorite designers!

CHAPTER 7

Accessories: The Bold Final Touch

Accessories can pull your entire wardrobe together, update your look, and provide the finishing touches to any basic dress or suit. You can buy beautiful quality clothes, but it takes a sense of style and imagination to coordinate your accessories well to make the fashion impression you want.

Accessories make your wardrobe seem larger. When you select the right ones for your season and your style, you make a high-fashion statement. Even if you are on a budget, a unique belt, a beautiful vest, or a bold pair of earrings will add a look of sophistication and style to your classic suit or dress. Accessories of quality and in your colors are a sound fashion statement and an investment you must continue to make as your career develops. It sounds difficult to choose the right jewelry, scarves, belts, shoes, and hats—but it's not if you know your season.

The Basic Black Dress

I recall wearing a basic black dress with a pair of black patent pumps and black opaque tights. To accessorize it, I wore a three-and-a-half-inch black patent belt and silver jewelry. I sold ten to twelve customers on that one basic dress, and helped them choose accessories to change the look in the following ways.

A Signature of Your Style

You, too, can add your own distinctive signature to your wardrobe with the right accessories. Many of you may own the same dress, but the way in which you complete your look provides the distinctive signature—your signature of style. When you use accessories creatively, you express yourself and create a lasting impression on those you meet.

Jewelry

Jewelry should add to your glamour and style and balance your fashion statement. It is the most important accessory you can purchase, and it expresses your personality.

Autumns are romantic, earthy women and generally are attracted to large ethnic or high-fashion jewelry. Gold works well for the Autumn woman of color. Winters are dramatic and attracted to bold, modern, one-of-a-kind jewelry. Silver and crystal look very striking on Winters.

Summers are usually classic women who prefer wearing their favorite pieces over and over again. They can be found wearing white pearls, understated watches, and stud earrings that match their necklaces. Springs are usually sporty types who don't like much jewelry. They need only a gold watch and gold earrings to feel well dressed. For a funky look, however, they choose jewelry of colored stones.

Purchasing expensive pieces of jewelry can be wonderful if you can afford to take the risk of wearing them: people may notice your jewelry rather than you. To me, these are too much of a status symbol. And wearing too much at one time can be a mistake. Custom jewelry seems to be most appropriate in the 1990s because women are more aware of who they are, and are less concerned by how many pieces of jewelry they can wear. But for those who want to wear the real thing, here are some suggestions. For Springs, pearls and a gold chain hung together are elegant. For a tall Autumn, lots of pearls and several stoned gold chains can work well. Summers are happy in pearls alone, while Winters look great in diamonds.

Handbags

Handbags are important elements of dressing for success. You should select one to go with your shoes, but keep your life-style and profession in mind as well. The slim envelope bag may look stylish, but does it hold enough? The large handbag may hold everything you own, but does it look too clunky, or out of proportion with your tailored suit?

Purchase your theme color purse before you buy accessory color purses. Spend a bit more for the theme purse, since it should go with almost anything. A black purse is a good choice for Winters and Summers, brown or camel for Autumns and Springs. These colors will complement the colors in your wardrobe. When buying a purse for the year's cooler seasons, take or wear your coat to coordinate it with your selection.

Shoes

I find shoes *fascinating*. Some are unique works of art with platforms, delicate and intricate straps, and expressive heels; others are beautiful simply because they are elegant flats that complete your day or evening outfit.

If you have nice legs, and medium-width feet, almost any type of shoe will look wonderful on you. But if you have a problem with the shape or size of your legs and the width of your feet, you will have to select a shoe more carefully. For example, ankle straps overemphasize heavy legs or thick ankles. If you have either of these problems, purchase shoes that are cut low in the front; if possible, nearly all should have a closed toe. This will give an illusion of length to your leg and will be sexy and alluring.

Boots are flattering on most women and can be used to disguise a multitude of flaws. Be very careful in purchasing boots, and try to buy quality, the very best you can afford. Treat them well and they will be with you a lot longer than a shoe or pump. Boots are an investment and add that tailored or western appeal to longer skirts and leggings.

It is important to buy shoes, like handbags, in theme colors because they will work with everything in your closet. Summers and Winters should own at least one excellent pair of black pumps; Autumns and Springs, brown or camel leather pumps.

If you are purchasing a special pair of shoes for a particular outfit and the shoes will match other items in your closet, buy *two* pairs. You will need that extra pair for the next season.

Hats

Selecting hats can be great fun, especially if you go with your best friend. You can browse from hat to hat and try on whatever is available. Make sure the brim and crown are the right size for your face, hairstyle, body size, and shape. A large hat on a short woman can be overpowering; on a tall woman, a tiny hat can disappear. It is very

important to use a full-length mirror so that you make sure the hat is proportioned to your size.

Wearing a hat can be lots of fun, but choose carefully *where* you wear one. It's not appropriate in many work places to wear a hat all day. If you are in the arts, public relations, advertising, or even journalism, you can get by with wearing a hat all day. But if you are in a law, financial, or medical office or in the classroom or the boardroom all day, you will want to remove the hat when you go inside and leave the fun for after work.

Scarves

Scarves serve as accents to the basic items in your wardrobe. Use them to show off your sense of style and personality. Because scarves have movement and a personality of their own, they can complement your basic wardrobe and add pizzazz. When you select a scarf, be sure the colors are in your palette so it will coordinate with numerous outfits. There are scores of ways to tie a scarf—some are formal, others are free. Remember: *A knot can do a lot.*

Eyeglasses

Wearing glasses may be a necessity, but they can be worn just for fun as an important fashion accessory and an expression of your personality. My advice to you is to select a frame that is in proportion to your face. Pay close attention to its color and design. Those with oval faces may wear any shape frame. Square frames are best for round faces, and long faces should sport large lenses, but ones no wider than the face. Round glasses look great on oval and diamond-shaped faces.

If your eyes are close-set, choose a smaller frame. If you have wide-set eyes, a larger frame will be a lot more flattering.

And, when selecting frames, make sure you consider your Season:

Women of Winter—blues, burgundy, and silver

Women of Summer—blues and grays

Women of Autumn—brown and tortoise

Women of Spring—beige and gold

If you color your hair, don't forget to coordinate the color of your frames to your *season* and not to hair which (heaven forbid!) may have been colored incorrectly. *Change your hair color, not your glasses.*

Hosiery

Hosiery completes any outfit. Here is a simple guide to the right shades for your season.

Women of Winter—neutral, navy, black, taupe, or white

Women of Summer—taupe, off-white, or neutral

Women of Autumn—ivory, brown, ash, khaki, or almond

Women of Spring—ivory, nude, beige, or sand

Fragrances

For me, perfume is like a lingering impression, a scent that mixes with the air as you are walking away. The scent will always say, "I've been there and I am feeling great." Did you know that your memory of smell is more accurate and lasting than any other sense?

Selecting perfume is such a direct route to the unconscious that it can become a personal signature. So choose your fragrance carefully, and don't rush the process. What may smell wonderful on your friend may not have the same effect on you because of your body chemistry.

Recently I was feeling low and thought I needed to change my fragrance. The change adversely affected my mood, style, and sense of dressing. Each morning, as I dressed, I bathed myself in my new fragrance and started the selection process for what to wear for the day. My style changed and so did my attitude. I stayed with this fragrance for one week, but by the end of the week I was a wreck. It was the wrong fragrance. I switched back to the fragrance I had been wearing for some time and my life came back into perspective. Each of us has a different chemical balance that reacts to perfumes and colognes. Take your time in selecting and decide on a fragrance that makes you feel like the woman you are.

Sweet florals, which have a soft, feminine smell, are best suited to Summers and Springs. For example, Summers may prefer White Linen while Springs may enjoy the fragrance of Giorgio. Exotic fragrances are rich and spicy and appeal to Winters and Autumns. Winters may like White Diamonds by Elizabeth Taylor, and Autumns may find Bijou and Opium appealing.

Note: Perfume has a life span of three years, so it is not wise to purchase too much at one time.

The Faces of the Seasons

*F*or many women, putting on makeup is like painting an image of themselves. It's creative. It's exciting to see the transformation right before your eyes. And soon, when you've learned to use the makeup colors in your palette, it will be easy for you to develop your own look that reflects your natural beauty. The first rule is that your makeup should enhance the coolness or the warmness of your skin, hair, and eyes — just as your clothes and accessories should.

Anita

Anita is a cool Winter who knows that the bold, clear makeup colors of the Winter palette bring out all her natural drama and vivacity.

Yolande

Yolande is a warm Spring who has discovered that the light, bright makeup colors of the Spring palette always enhance her delicate, blooming beauty.

Tomara

Tomara is so pretty that even in Winter's cool colors she looks good. But notice how the dark blue is a little overwhelming for her delicate good looks, and so is the more dramatic makeup. She's sophisticated, but does she look a little too mature? In her light, bright yellow, Tomara is a true daffodil Spring — full of sunshine and warmth. Her skin glows, and her makeup enhances her youthfulness and grace.

Heather

Heather can wear butterscotch, but it bleaches the color from her face, despite her warm Autumn makeup, and makes her look a little tired and sallow. Heather is really a breezy Summer, absolutely soft and rosy in her pretty cranberry blouse and cool Summer makeup. The muted pinks and roses give her the gentle beauty we appreciate in Summers.

Skin Care

Three Steps to Cleaner, Softer Skin

(1) Proper cleansing keeps your complexion free of impurities. All cleansing products should have a gentle stimulating effect on your skin.

(2) A Toner stimulates a healthy glow and removes any impurities that remain after cleansing.

(3) Protection retards early wrinkles. Only use a moisturizer designed for your skin: oily, normal, or dry. But everyone should drink water, plenty of water.

Tools for Cleaner, Softer Skin

All of these should be designed for your skin — oily, normal, or dry:

(1) Cleanser to get your skin squeaky clean;

(2) Toner to remove impurities and stimulate a healthy glow;

(3) Moisturizer to protect your skin and guard against early aging.

Concealer

Concealers help disguise flaws, bags, and discoloration under the eye area. They come in various shades, so be sure to select a color that blends well with your foundation. If you have dry skin, use a cream instead of the popular cover sticks. Use a fine-tipped makeup brush to apply the concealer, then the foundation, and blend into the trouble area.

Concealer Colors

Warm   Cool

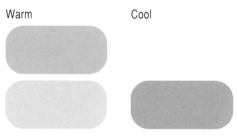

Foundation

Eyes

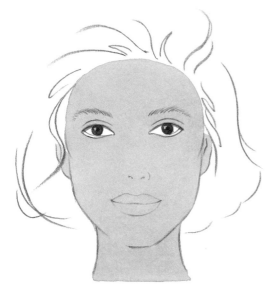

Your foundation should be neither too dark, nor too light, and should, of course, complement the warm or cool undertones of your complexion. Dab foundation on your forehead, cheeks, nose, chin, and eyelids.

Using a dampened triangle sponge, spread and blend it downward and out in long quick strokes. Apply a translucent powder to even and tone your skin and set your foundation.

Eye color is a good way to contour and highlight your eyes—the most important feature on your face. Remember that the eye area is the most delicate area of your face. Make sure your eye pencils are neither too sharp nor too dull. Start by applying foundation to your eyelids.

Eyeliner

Use an eyeliner or eye pencil to add dimension and depth to your eyes. Start at the center of your eye; draw a fine line to the outer corner, always staying under your lashes.

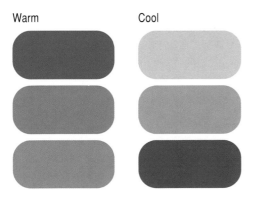

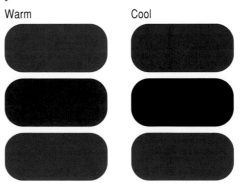

Eye Shadow

Smooth your primary eye shadow to the outer edge of the lid and blend toward the crease.

Warm   Cool

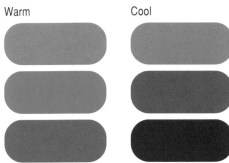

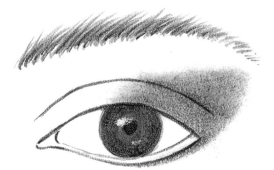

Mascara

Mascara gives your eyes intensity by making them appear thicker and longer. Apply the first coat on one eye and then proceed with coating the other. Go back and forth between your eyes two to three times, holding your mascara wand in your lashes.

Warm   Cool

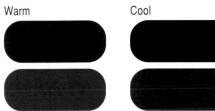

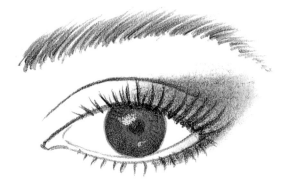

Eye Pencil

To set your eye makeup, apply small angular strokes of color at the outer edge of your eyelids with an eyeliner pencil.

Warm   Cool

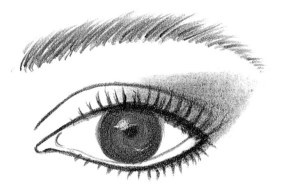

Eyebrows

Blush

Eyebrows frame your eyes and will enhance their beauty when "groomed" to their natural shape. They should always be kept in proportion to the rest of your features. Avoid heavy painted lines above your brows. Color them naturally by making tiny strokes along the inside curve of your brow.

If your brows meet over your nose, tweeze the excess hair. Using a waxing technique is also effective for shaping them naturally.

If your brows are "wild," brush on a little brow control gel to keep them in control all day long.

For skimpy brows, use a pencil or brow powder to fill in the gap.

Start the application of blush near the little flap in the center of your ear; sweep the color inward over the apple of your cheek and softly blend. The idea is to look slightly flushed, not painted.

Warm   Cool

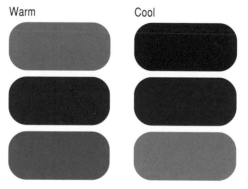

Warm   Cool

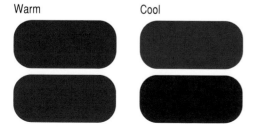

Lips

Second only to your eyes, your lips and mouth are the most expressive features on your face. Depending on the size of your lips and your own personal preference, you may choose to emphasize or de-emphasize this feature. All women of color should wear lipstick.

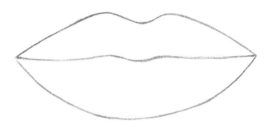

Outline your lips with a pencil that is the same color or close to the color of your lipstick. Then, apply your lipstick straight from the case.

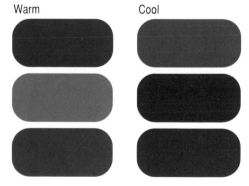

Voilà!

Cool

Warm

On the left is a Cool face, and on the right a Warm face. These illustrations have a lighter skin tone so that you can see more easily the different undertones — warm vs. cool. Notice how Cool's complexion is more pink, Warm's more golden.

Also notice how the foundation, eye shadow, blush, and lipstick colors go together to create a coordinated look and a unified color balance.

You can clearly see how making the right determination of your undertone is the first step to creating your best look!

Now that you've learned what colors are best for you and how to apply them, go out and become an artist. Remember, skin care is vital and all the makeup in the world won't hide a neglected complexion.

Between salon visits, try some natural beauty pick-me-ups to keep your skin healthy. Lemon and witch hazel are great as oily skin astringents. Tea bags pressed gently under your eyes relieve puffiness. Most important: drink eight to ten glasses of water a day to renew your system and keep your skin soft and well hydrated.

CHAPTER 8

Create a New You with Makeup

"Mirror, Mirror on the wall ..." You know the rest of the question, and the answer is: you. Too often, we look in the mirror and begin a futile process, one in which we should never indulge. We begin to apply makeup to try to fit an image from a magazine or to copy the look of someone else. When we do this, we make a big mistake. No matter how beautiful another woman may be, you don't really want to look like her. You want to enhance and make more beautiful what is you. The object is to work with what nature has given you, blending colors that reflect who you really are.

When the Artist Looks in the Mirror

Have you heard the expression "beating your face for points"? It is an expression that refers to the very old habit of patting and squeezing the skin a little to bring natural color to the skin's surface. Well, the result is similar to what you see when a woman is wearing makeup and her natural beauty can be seen through the cosmetics and colors she applied.

This chapter is going to give you advice on selecting and applying your makeup, but first we must prepare and take care to preserve the perfect canvas for our face art. The canvas, of course, is your skin.

Many makeup artists and department store sales representatives begin by offering you makeup and eventually work around to skin care. This is putting the proverbial cart before the horse. We are going to begin at the beginning; our first concern is the proper care of your skin.

Skin Care

Every day your skin is faced with dirt, dust, pollution, sun, and wind—and it reflects your inner thoughts. Your face is the landscape of all of your thoughts and feelings. Depression, worry, and anxiety become a part of your facial expression, just as joy and happiness are reflected there and can keep you looking youthful well into old age. But good thoughts aside, in coming to terms with age, a skin care regimen is essential.

In order to have good skin, you must first make sure that your skin is receiving all the nourishment it needs, including plenty of protein to help its cells renew themselves. In addition to a proper diet, your skin needs help in three other very important ways, and that's where cosmetic science really helps.

1. Proper **cleansing** keeps your complexion free of impurities. All cleansing products should have a gentle stimulating effect on your skin.

2. A good **toner** stimulates a healthy glow and removes any impurities that remain after cleansing.

3. **Protection** retards early wrinkles. Use a moisturizer designed specifically for your skin type, and drink water, plenty of water.

As you may know, there are three skin types:

❑ **Normal skin** has no shine, has clear tone, and is soft and supple but not greasy or uncomfortable to the touch;

❑ **Oily skin** is very shiny and smooth to the touch, with visibly enlarged pores, but because it retains moisture, it tends to remain youthful;

❑ **Dry skin** has no shine, is characterized by flakes or dry patches, and is very easily irritated. The skin tone is thin and needs moisturizers to reduce the propensity toward wrinkles.

The Care and Feeding of Your Complexion

Here are some helpful at-home hints to make your visits to the skin care specialist less frequent and less costly.

1. Between visits, use health food beauty pick-me-ups.

    • Use either lemon juice or witch hazel as an oily skin astringent. Apply with a cotton pad.

    • Apply cool, damp tea bags as compresses to puffiness around the eyes; they work better than herbals.

    • Citrus and acidic fruits such as strawberries, lemon, papaya, tomato and grapefruit are good for oily skin. Blend one or two together in a blender, and apply the juice with a cotton pad to your face after cleansing.

    • Used as a paste-like facial mask, bananas, avocados, and pears stimulate moisture in dry skin. Apply the paste to your face, let stand for ten minutes, then wash, alternating warm and cool water to tighten the pores.

2. Drink eight to ten glasses of natural water a day to renew and cleanse your system and keep your skin soft and well hydrated.

3. Vitamin E is good for lightening the darkness under tired eyes and adding moisture.

4. Avoid such stimulants as tea, coffee, chocolate, and alcohol.

5. To create a new you, set aside one day a week that is *just for you;* indulge yourself with a facial, manicure, or pedicure.

Makeup

Makeup should be applied so skillfully that it enhances your natural beauty and draws attention to the uniqueness of your features. If you apply makeup only to disguise what you consider your flaws, you are making a *big* mistake.

Nowadays I concentrate on enhancing my eyes and lips, for instance, because they give my face drama. I was not always confident about my dramatic features because I didn't know who I was and how to work with what God had given me. Today I'm happy with what I thought were flaws because I learned a few simple cosmetic techniques and the best colors to enhance my good features, and I want to share those with you.

To begin, remember it is important to develop *your* own look. No matter how beautiful another woman may appear to be, you really don't want to look like her. You want to enhance and make more beautiful what is *you*.

Now that you've learned what colors are best for you, let's apply the color theory to makeup just for you.

Romantic and dramatic Winters—cool, bold, clear colors

Sporty and classic Summers—cool, muted colors

Sophisticated and preppy Autumns—deep, warm earth tones

Glamorous and fun-loving Springs—warm, bright colors

Practicality

How many times have you purchased a foundation or lipstick, or even a blush, thinking that it looks great on you, then leave the store, glance in the rear view mirror, and suddenly you don't recognize the person who is staring back at you? The makeup you purchased doesn't match your skin tone or your personality!

I am sure you have accumulated a cabinet full of makeup in the wrong colors over the years. Well, it's time for a little practicality. If you make your next makeup purchase according to the colors I have developed for you, you'll never have this problem again.

Foundation

Also called base, foundation covers minor flaws, hides blemishes and freckles, and evens your skin color. It also lays the groundwork for all of the wonderful colors in your palette. Some foundations are tinted, and most cosmetic manufacturers are developing colors especially for women of color.

If you purchase a foundation that is too dark or too light, you will have a cast or washed-out tone to the skin. A foundation should complement your skin's undertone. Complexions fall into four categories:

- cool and deep

- cool and pink

- warm and rich

- warm and bright

To test a foundation, apply a dab to your jaw *only*. Don't apply to cheeks, nose, or chin because these areas are usually a bit darker than the rest of your face. If you are not certain to which category you belong, take your makeup palette with you when making a purchase. If you are still in doubt, I recommend custom-blended foundations. Custom blending ensures a more polished look for women of color.

Also remember to select a foundation that it is geared to your skin's moisture content. If your skin is oily, an oil-free or water-based makeup will help minimize the oil, especially in the T-zone (the space between your eyes, forehead, and nose). Oily skin makes maintaining a matte, fresh look difficult. Because it takes only a few hours for the oils to seep through, causing your foundation to fade and discolor, you must be sure to purchase an oil-free product.

If you have dry skin, use a moisture-rich foundation in cream or liquid form.

Normal or combination skin means that your skin is very oily in the T-zone and drier on the cheek area. Remember that combination skin will change with seasons, becoming drier in winter and oilier during the summer months.

If you have blemished or acne-prone skin, you will need to be even more careful and scrupulous about your cosmetic needs. This skin type is usually oily, so always *prime* the skin with an astringent before applying a foundation; this will tighten the pores and create a smooth, matte finish. Also, look for labels that say "non-comedogenic," which means they are less harsh and abrasive.

If your skin is sensitive, your makeup should be hypoallergenic, which means allergy tested or specially developed for sensitive skin. Avoid cosmetics that list lanolin and alcohol as the primary ingredients.

Use **concealers** to disguise flaws, bags, and discoloration under the eyes. Concealers come in various shades, so be sure to select a color that blends well with your foundation. If you have dry skin, choose a cream instead of the popular cover sticks. Invest in a fine-tipped makeup brush for application. First apply your foundation, then take the concealer and blend it into any trouble area to conceal pimples or spots.

Application of the foundation is definitely an art. Women of color want to use it to enhance their complexion, not to serve as a mask. Follow these three steps in applying the foundation.

1. Dab the foundation on the forehead, cheeks, nose, chin, and eyelids.

2. Using a dampened triangle sponge, spread and blend the foundation downward and out in long quick strokes.

3. Use a translucent powder over the face and neck to set the foundation. Apply loose powder with a fluffy brush or cotton puff. If you use a compact translucent powder, pat it on with a puff, making

sure the action should be in the wrist, not the puff. Also, be sure to change your puff once every seven days depending on skin type; replacement of puffs is especially important if you have oily skin.

Powder

Many women who have skin that is particularly even and free of inconsistencies do not need foundation to tone their skin. They need only a tinted translucent powder. When used over foundation, however, powder softens the appearance of makeup.

If your skin is dry, use a moisturizing powder from a pressed compact. If your skin is oily, an oil-absorbing loose powder will best suit your complexion. Normal or combination skin can be enhanced with either loose or pressed powder.

Here are four powdering techniques that will help your makeup remain radiant throughout the day. But always remember to use loose powder *lightly* and *gently*, and don't overdo.

1.   A little loose powder will change your lipstick from shiny to matte. Apply your lip color, then dust loose translucent powder over your lips with a small fluffy brush.

2.   Dip a cotton swab into loose powder and gently brush your eyelids before applying eyeliner. This will keep your liner from running.

3.   To blend your cheek color, apply foundation, then translucent powder with a fluffy blush brush. Next apply cheek color, and seal with translucent powder.

4. To blend eye shadow, dust loose translucent powder over the shadow with medium size fluffy blush brush. This will give the shadow a matte finish.

For Your Eyes Only

Mascara gives the eyes intensity. Here are the best colors for each season.

Winter—darkest brown to black

Summer—charcoal to darkest brown

Autumn—dark brown

Spring—brown

Applying Eye Color

Eye color is a good way to contour and highlight your eyes, and here are five steps to perfect eye makeup techniques. But first, remember that the eye area is the most delicate area of your face. To eliminate added pressure on this tender area, make sure your eye pencils are not too sharp or dull. Also, reduce the possibility of eye infections by sharpening your pencils often to remove bacteria that have settled on them.

1. Apply foundation to your eyelids.

2. Use an eyeliner or eye pencil to add dimension and depth to your eyes. Starting at the center of your eye, draw a fine line to the outer corner, always staying *under* your lashes.

3. Smooth your primary color eye shadow to the outer edge of the lid and blend toward the crease.

4. If you employ mascara for thicker, longer lashes, apply your first coat on one eye and proceed with coating the other. Go back and forth two to three times, each time running the wand through the curves of the lashes. Then apply one coat of mascara to the bottom lashes.

5. Finish by using a colored eye pencil to make a soft line along the outer edge of your upper and lower lids.

Eye Shadow and Eyebrows

Of all the makeup tools, eye shadow is the most like paint. Often packaged in small palettes, it comes in powder or cream form. I find powders, which come with applicators, are the easiest to apply, but if you have dry skin, a cream shadow is better.

Eye shadow should be applied to the eyelid first, then blended to sculpture the entire eye. Select the lightest color for the lid, then contour and accent your eye at the crease with a deeper color. The brow bone is best left natural, or you may choose one of your neutral colors.

Eyebrows frame your eyes and will enhance your beauty when groomed to their natural shape. Avoid heavy painted lines above your brows. Color them naturally by making tiny strokes along the inside curve of the brow.

To test the proportion of your eyebrows, hold a pencil vertically along the line of your nose. If your brow line crosses over to the edge of your nose, tweeze the excess hair.

A new waxing technique is also effective for shaping them naturally. If your brows are wild, brush on a little brow control gel to keep them in control all day long.

If your brows are skimpy or fail to reach the vertical line along your nose, use a pencil or brow powder to fill in the gap.

Blush or Cheek Color

Your cheek color should be applied with a fat, soft-bristled blush brush, after you apply foundation. Brush in a natural and even pattern. Blush gives a youthful appearance if applied properly. Base your blush color on your makeup color palette:

Winters—true red and shocking pink

Summers—cool red, clear pink, and rose

Autumns—orange-red and deep peach

Springs—coral and peach

Start the application of your blush near the little flap in the center of your ear; then sweep color inward over the cheek's apple and softly blend to emphasize your cheek's structure and create a slightly flushed look.

Lipstick/Lip Liner

I could write an entire chapter on lipstick from the experiences I've had over the years. Second only to your eyes, your lips and mouth are the most expressive features on your face. Depending on the size of your lips and your own personal preference, you may choose to emphasize or play down this feature. Many women of color choose not to use the other kinds of makeup discussed in this chapter, but *all* should wear lip color. How should you apply it? I apply mine straight from the holder. I don't use a lip brush, but I do outline my lips with a pencil that is the same color or close to my lipstick color.

Hands and Nails

Your hands and nails are very important to your total image. They add the final touch and when neglected make you seem older or less polished than you are. They are on display all the time and tell the world how you really feel about yourself.

Because I own a full-service beauty and skin care salon, my hands are in water and chemicals much of the day. I've experienced my share of embarrassing moments. One evening I had to attend a black tie dinner. All I had time to do was to shower, put on my makeup and my dress, and run out the door. My hands were a wreck, so I tried to polish over the chipped nail polish as I was driving. Well, I spilled that red polish on my dress and ruined it. You can imagine what happened to my evening!

That episode was very costly. The following day I had my manicurist apply a coating of acrylic over my natural nails. With this done, I don't have to polish my nails every day. Now when I need to be at a special event or want my polish to look fresh, I just use a clear top coat. Now let's go over some basic hand and nail tips that can help you maintain a total look, despite your busy schedule. Don't let me hear you say, "I have no nails." You *can* have them. Nails are like flowers: Feed them, nourish them, and they'll grow! With a regular manicure every seven to ten days, your nails and hands will look and feel great in no time.

Each nail should be shaped or cut to the same length. Your nail color should match your lipstick and blush colors from your season's palette. If you don't color your nails, wear a clear protective polish to create that well-groomed look you need.

And don't forget diet. It has a *lot* to do with your nails. When your diet lacks the proper nutrition, your nails can break and split much more easily.

Use a rich moisturizer throughout the day, especially after you wash your hands. Moisturizers not only keep you hands smooth and pliant but also are great for your cuticles.

So even if your hands are not long and slender and your nails are short, moisturize, shape, and polish for that professional image you need on the job.

Foot Care

Your feet are the most abused part of your body. With the weight we put on them, the walking that we do, and our tight shoes, it's no wonder that they hurt.

Have you ever purchased a pair of shoes in size seven and a half when you wear a size eight and a half? I'm sure we all have spotted that adorable pair of shoes we just had to have, no matter what size we had to squeeze our poor feet into. We dance out in them that evening, but soon we have to sit down and take those gorgeous shoes off under the table. The next day our feet are still burning and sore. The lesson is obvious: *Always wear shoes that fit.* Another good lesson for us working women is to vary the height of our heels each day.

And, just because your feet are always covered, is no reason they shouldn't be just as pretty as the rest of you. It's time to begin scheduling a regular pedicure, if you haven't done so. After you've had your first one, you may think a pedicure is the answer to all your problems. While they certainly won't take care of your taxes, they can make you and your feet feel and look a lot better. They are just as important as a manicure to your health and well-being. You should schedule a pedicure every ten to twenty days, depending on your life-style, especially if you exercise a lot.

Here are some tips for in between:

- If you suffer from dry feet, massage a heavy moisturizer or petroleum jelly into them before you go to sleep at night.

- Keep your toenails cut short and straight across, to prevent hang nails and snagged hosiery.

- When you buy shoes, make sure they are the right fit. You should be able to wiggle your toes. Whatever you do, don't purchase those gotta-have-'em pumps if they don't fit. Poorly fitting shoes can cause bunions, corns and warts—hardly appropriate to our image as sophisticated ladies.

Keep your feet well manicured, and you can wear those slinky high heels or pointed suede shoes occasionally, and even step out in those strappy sandals he likes so much. Treat your feet well and walk in confidence.

A New Beginning

Bonita came to me in search of what she called a middle-age re-vamping of hair, makeup, and wardrobe. Bonita was 50 years old and beginning to feel, as she termed it, "like a middle-aged frump." Although she is a registered nurse and nurturing comes second nature to her, she needed some nurturing herself.

I gave her a color analysis and we discovered that she is a Summer. We developed a fresh new makeup look and added under-eye cream to help retard the fine lines around her eyes and restore her skin. We developed a diet and exercise program to fit her life-style. Because she had recently lost weight, I gave her a contouring body cream to help tighten and firm her legs and thighs and another skin cream to tone and tighten the skin on her neck. I consider these body creams part of the total makeover treatment for my clients.

Bonita felt rejuvenated, and looked and felt younger than her years. How about you?

CHAPTER 9

Coming to Terms
with Self and Age

Aging is a very spiritual journey. We spend most of lives ignoring
the journey we take through life when it is the most important trip
we'll make. Because our society equates everything with money, we
believe that only money can preserve our youthful appearance. We
believe we must spend a million to look like a million. This premise is
simply not true.

Aging gracefully is a process involving self-motivation, self-
respect, and, the greatest of all, self-love. Your face and carriage, your
entire presence, should reflect your loving, giving, and sharing.

Love Yourself

When you were a baby, your mother gave you the basic recipe for
helping you to conquer the world; she taught you self-love. It was
passed to her from the generation before, and she passed it to you. But
now as a maturing adult woman, you must continue the journey with
less guidance than you had before. It's a little frightening, but also it's
exciting. With self-assurance, the confidence you've gained from life's
experiences, and the sense of your own beauty that your colors give
you, you can return to the road of life with new zest and a sense of
adventure.

Here's what the woman of color needs to create inner beauty.

1. **Self-confidence.** Confidence is difficult to define, but we all know it when we see it. Sometimes it is a woman walking proudly down the street who attracts our eye although she is not a model. Self-confidence implies, to me, a balance between self-control and courage. True confidence is marked by simplicity and sincerity and comes with age, experience, and adversity. Adversity is the greatest of all because it means rebuilding your character.

2. **Discipline and patience.** The difference between a beautiful woman and an average woman is discipline. In fact, discipline is the great equalizer. If a woman is beautiful but lacks discipline, it shows in her expression. A woman who may be considered plain but who is disciplined and patient has facial expressions that appear beautiful and refined.

   Daily attention to beauty routine is one side of discipline. The other is attention to nutrition, hair care, skin care, makeup, and, of course, fashion. Fashion is an important part of your daily routine. Pick up any fashion magazine and you'll read about a revolutionary makeup or cosmetic that will make you look younger longer. You'll find lots of helpful hints for women over forty. You don't have to be a scientist or beauty consultant to know about the latest beauty trends; just having an open mind and a healthy outlook on life will keep you up-to-date.

3. **Attitude.** Here we have one of the most important keys to success. Our attitude toward others, our goals, accomplishments and setbacks, and yes, life itself, can be the measure of our success. A successful woman who does not have a positive attitude has not really succeeded. She may be capable of commanding audiences,

but it is highly unlikely that she is capable of commanding respect. We are all drawn to those who exude a positive outlook and shun others who do not. We are inclined to respect a woman whose approach is a positive one.

4. **Daring and imagination.** Allow yourself to think about the future, and imagine what it holds for you. You may imagine a retirement community. Perhaps your vision of the future includes days in the sun on a golf course or tennis court. Or, perhaps you imagine whiling away the hours with good books in a cabin in the woods.

Whatever you envision, you probably sense that your experiences along the way will help shape what the future will hold. Perhaps the experiences were from the old school of hard knocks, or perhaps, you attribute them to careful planning. The truth is, aging is a thought process that ultimately crosses the span of time.

Living through the 1980s and 1990s and walking slowly into the year 2000, I have found some basics to be true. One is that stress accounts for many of the illnesses women suffer. I am not a physician, but I know that stress takes its toll, and because its roots are mental, stress can be controlled.

In this chapter, we are going to create and explore a new way for aging gracefully. Here are eleven ways that have helped me through my own journey.

1. **Read for guidance and comfort.** Journalist Ida B. Wells-Barnett, poet Maya Angelou, India's Indira Gandhi, Israel's Golda Meir, labor activist Cesar Chavez, South Africa's Winnie Mandela, magazine editor Susan Taylor (*In the Spirit*), artist Diana Ross (*Life of the Sparrow*), and many others have guided me through my

journey. I am fortified by reading about people of color. Through their autobiographies and work, I share their life experiences. I listen to them as they transcend the years between us, providing me with inspiration and new heroes. Their stories relate their sources of strength, and help me to clarify my own perspective. Exploring their thoughts and learning what inspired them helps to keep me going. Reading about their determination and spirit has been an anchor and a friend for me.

2. **Meditate in the morning.** Sunday school? No. It is simply the perfect way to begin each day. Allow yourself time each morning for clearing your mind of everything. The morning works best, because often you wake up without the full list of the day's tasks on your mind. Take this time to think only of the spiritual you, that part of you that you find most difficult to reach during a hectic day and most easy to love when you give her a little time.

    Use this time to ask the higher power to continue to create direction for you so that you can continue on the right path. I also ask for wisdom, knowing that wisdom is the key to unlocking all my strength and potential for success.

3. **Eliminate the negative and affirm the positive.** Eliminating negative thoughts and people from your path can revolutionize your day. When I find people and tasks closing in on me during the course of the day, I take a few minutes away from it all to regain control. I list the positive things in my life and mentally repeat positive thoughts. Positive thinking is the only way we can stay on the road to building self-love, respect, and harmony.

    I make a special effort to remove all negative thoughts, and, most of all, I refuse to listen to anything negative around me. Deciding that you and only you are the most important person in your life, and repeating that decision to yourself, can help remove negative situations from your day. Once you've done this, you can visualize where you are headed and how to get there.

We can create negative light and wallow in it, or we can create positive light and allow its energy to create for us a life of happiness. From the positive light, we can derive hope, and hope can provide us with the thrust we need to meet our goals.

4. **Pass on the "have-tos."** Every day is full of things you have to accomplish. Because you are determined to complete those things you see as priorities, you become all things to all people. As women of color, we are taught to get the job done. We are taught that duty comes first, and so we commit ourselves to completing the tasks no matter how daunting they are. We make the time to get the job done. Far be it from me to suggest you procrastinate, but isn't there someone who can help you? Learn how to delegate duties and responsibilities that you think only you can handle. The truth is, you probably have a few people who can help with the myriad of errands and tasks you've assigned to yourself. And look at it this way; with a little practice, those people are probably capable of completing the tasks as well as you.

5. **To work well, eat well.** Nutrition is important to our mental and physical well-being. Certainly, you've heard of brain food! Eating the right foods—such as five helpings of fruits and vegetables every day—will help you to think clearly and provide the energy you need to accomplish the day's tasks. You must take the time to eat the foods that will help you refuel.

6. **Have a perfect ending to every day.** Taking an end-of-the-day vacation each evening before you retire will work wonders for your psyche and your body. This tranquil time is for you to unwind and release yourself of all the day's woes. Allot time each evening just for you. Notice I said **allot**, not steal. Don't allow yourself to believe this time belongs somewhere else, or to some task left undone. This will bring on guilt. (And you *know* how we women love to take on guilt!) Instead, say to yourself, "I *deserve* these few minutes."

   Find a quiet place after your day is complete. Contemplate. But don't confuse contemplating with listing your problems and tasks and trying to resolve them. Think about yourself instead. Give some time to your spirit. This is the time during which you give your spirit a chance to rule and guide the rest of you.

7. **Meditate each evening.** Meditation helps relax and energize your body, mind, and soul. Use your bathtub as your spa. Spa essentials are:

- Music (whatever you like best: jazz, love songs, opera, etc.)

- Your favorite nonalcoholic drink

- Scented bath oil, gels, soap, or bubble bath

- Exfoliant to remove dead skin cells

- Facial mask

- Eye pads

- Bath pillow

Pack a bag with your spa essentials and take it with you to the bathroom. Turn on the water and fill that tub with warm, sweet-smelling calm. Baths are the number one stress-relief remedy, especially for women of color who are busy changing the world through juggling their career, family, and social life.

A spa bath allows you to distance yourself from the normal wear and tear of becoming a more successful woman of color. Giving yourself this pampering allows you to pull yourself back together again and be calmer, more thoughtful, and more relaxed than when you entered the bathroom.

8. **Set short-term, attainable goals.** Make short-term goals for yourself. I find sixty- to ninety-day goals work best because they don't add additional pressure to an already stressful schedule. Long-term goals—without any short-term ones in between—can make you feel tense and anxious because you don't know where to begin.

9. **Provide closure.** Have you ever told someone "maybe" because you didn't want to hurt his or her feelings, or you didn't want to make a decision? In these situations, which are often unpleasant, you walk away, leaving the door open to revisiting the same issue much too soon. Over the years I have found putting topics and issues to rest is the best policy. If the opportunity presents itself, make the decision: Say yes or no. This will help you to move on to the next challenge. Adopting this philosophy demonstrates real growth.

10. **Dream.** Take a daydream break twice a week. Place yourself where you would like to be. This exercise will help you stay focused. We can easily become distracted from our goals by taking a wrong

turn and not knowing how to get back on track. This mental exercise is just as easy as it sounds: All it takes is discipline and a desire to be successful.

11. **Find time to reinvigorate the inner you.** "All of this sounds great," you say. "But do I really have time for this?" The answer is an unequivocal yes!

I live a busy and productive life. I play at least ten different roles for at least twenty different people. But I don't let time work against me. Because I spend time with the spiritual me, I am happy. I don't dole out time to myself in little spurts anymore. I give more freely of myself to myself.

Stop living by the philosophy of delayed gratification. Stop planning for the day when your work is complete. If you are good at what you do, your work may never be complete. Instead, take more time for yourself and use those times as rewards for the time already spent in successful work.

Defining the Process of Aging

At one point in writing this chapter, I had to look in the dictionary for the meaning of age. Like many words, it has many different definitions. And different women interpret age differently. The definition I like best is the idea of ripening to maturity. What does this mean to you? Does it mean there is a time limit to our mental and physical self or being? Is there a period when we stop growing and aging? No, because the spirit is within. It's a process that goes on *forever*. It's a process that says time waits for no one.

As a young girl, I knew that I was touched by the spirit of aging and self, but I didn't know how. At twenty years old, I had visions of becoming a solid and positive woman, but I didn't know how. Life's experiences helped me to sort out all the thoughts and visions going on in my head. Now I know that the spirit molds you, shapes you, and remakes you into the divine woman you are supposed to be. Although we are different colors with different heritages and have different opportunities, we all have a spirit within that creates who we will become and ultimately whom we create to add to the world of positive people. If we stop for a moment and reflect on our mothers' mother, or our grandmothers' mothers, we will find a different breed of women who had a wealth of knowledge to give to the women of today.

I often reflect where I was at twenty, or thirty, and I thank my heavenly spirit for directing me on the road to self love. A lot of love and introspection went into this chapter. Love yourself enough to take advantage of the advice.

A Long Line of Beauties

Most of us do not spend much time reflecting on what we will look like as we get older. Perhaps we steal a glance at our mothers, grandmothers, or great-grandmothers, then look at our daughters and wonder what they will be like.

The face of a woman tells the world the kind of life she's lived and how she feels about her age. I've often noticed women over forty watching beautiful young women with pride. It is hard to believe that at one point we were there. We don't want to go back because time and experience have been valuable to us, and the true value of that experience is difficult to express. Because we are proud of ourselves, we can watch a young woman with delight, indulgence, and grace. If we are confident, we can look at a younger woman and be grateful we no longer need to go through some of the things youth demands. And we can look ahead to a time of planned freedom and contentment.

Being proud of your life experiences will help you to come to terms with age. I've enjoyed being thirty-eight and having gone through life's ever-changing cycles. Recently, I stopped for a moment and looked at my 18-year-old and reflected back twenty years. Oh, how I see myself in her. Then, I glanced at my nine-year-old and wondered what she will be like at twenty, thirty, or forty, and I smiled with so much pride and love. God has given me joy and two new beginnings. What can I do as a woman and role model to ensure my daughters and my daughters' daughters will age with the grace and wisdom that I want to pass on to them? I can teach them that there is real joy in learning new things as an adult. We bring so much to the process of life and new learning.

My daughters will probably have experiences that I never considered and will go so much farther because my generation and all those before me have paved the way for change and female independence. But this will happen only because their minds are open and willing to be challenged. The doors are open for us women of color— more opportunities than even our mothers ever dreamed were possible for us.

So, if you put on a little weight, find that your vision is not what it used to be, get stiff around the knees, and notice a few beauty lines around the eyes, don't despair. You, too, can open that sealed bottle of grace that aging has been passed to you.

Darlene Mathis is founder and president of Monday Mornings Hair Design, Inc., a full-service beauty salon in Washington, D.C., for professional women and men of all ethnic diversities and nationalities. One of the area's most respected experts in the field of hair design and professional image makeovers, Ms. Mathis's clients include not only professional, congressional and society women, but companies like Marriott and Bloomingdales. A former consultant for *Color Me Beautiful*, she lives with her two daughters in the Washington, D.C. area.

Index

Photography and Production Credits

Design and Production
Chris Wolf

Photography
Edgar Thompson

Makeup Styling
Matthew Van Leeuwen

Illustrations
Sachiko Kanai

Hairstyling
Patricia McKillop, courtesy, Redkin
Mikel Stevens
Willis "Marque" Washington
Naomi Wouton, styling assistant

Models
Marcia Griffith - Award Agency
Sandy Azurdia, Paula Braile,
Marcia Giffith, Jenny Shyn - Stars Castings
Karen Carey
Anita Cooke
Catherine Cushenberry
Elizabeth A. Cushenberry
Erica Cushenberry
Yolande Donaldson
Edda Dumont
Naomi Travis-Dunkenfield

Addis Edossa
Anna Howard
Heather Johnson
Mitta Kakkat
Altomease Kennedy
Darvine J. Noel
Prerana Parek
Collette Rampersaud
Tomara Redman
Anne Sheon

Special Thanks
Guanita Jackson
Jerry Phillips
Tina and Rockman Rahman
Grace Speights
Debra Tang

Learn More...

Use this convenient coupon to receive information on Darlene Mathis's "Women of Color" makeup and fabric swatches in your season ...

☐ *Yes!* Please send me information about "Women of Color" fabric swatches from my seasonal palette in an attractive black purse-size leather case, convenient for smart shopping.

    ___Winter   ___Autumn
    ___Summer   ___Spring

☐ *Yes!* Please send me information about "Women of Color" makeup kits in my seasonal palette, including two shades of blush, two shades of eye shadow, two shades of lipstick, all specially chosen for my particular season.

    ___Winter   ___Autumn
    ___Summer   ___Spring

NAME_____

ADDRESS_____

CITY_____STATE_____ZIP_____

SEND A SELF-ADDRESSED STAMPED ENVELOPE TO:

Darlene Mathis "Women of Color"
P.O. Box 1003
Silver Spring, Maryland 20910